THE **G**LOBE **R**EADER'S **C**OLLECTION

# STORIES WITH A TWIST

**GLOBE FEARON EDUCATIONAL PUBLISHER**
**A Division of Simon & Schuster**
Upper Saddle River, New Jersey

**Executive Editor:** Barbara Levadi
**Senior Editor:** Bernice Golden
**Editors:** Helene Avraham, Laura Baselice, Robert McIlwaine
**Editorial Assistant:** Kristen Shepos
**Product Development:** PubWorks, Inc.
**Production Manager:** Penny Gibson
**Senior Production Editor:** Linda Greenberg
**Production Editor:** Walt Niedner
**Marketing Manager:** Sandra Hutchison
**Electronic Page Production:** The Wheetley Company, Inc.
**Cover Design:** The Wheetley Company, Inc.
**Cover Art:** Unknown Artist's *Moonlight Seascape II* A.G.E.,
Spain,SuperStock, Inc.
**Illustrations:** Chuck Gonzales

# ACKNOWLEDGMENTS

Grateful acknowledgment is made to the following publishers, authors, and other copy-right holders:**Alfred A. Knopf, Inc.,** for Patricia C. McKissack, "The 11:59" from *The Dark Thirty: Southern Tales of the Supernatural* by Patricia C. McKissack, illustrated by Brian Pinkney. Text copyright ©1992 by Patricia C. McKissack. Illustrations copyright ©1992 by Brian Pinkney. **August House inc.,** for Roberta Simpson Brown, "The Wake-Up Call" from *Queen of the Cold-blooded Tales* by Roberta Simpson Brown. Copyright ©1993 by Roberta Simpson Brown. **Joanna Lewis Cole,** for Judith Gorog, "Those Three Wishes" from *A Taste for Quiet* by Judith Gorog. Copyright ©1988, Judith Gorog. **Dell Books, a division of Bantam Doubleday Dell Publishing Group, Inc.,** for Robert D. San Souci, "Sister Death and the Healer," from *More Short and Shivery Stories* by Robert D. San Souci. Illustrations by K. Coville and J. Rogers. Text copyright ©1994 by Robert B. San Souci. Illustrations copyright ©1994 by Katherine Coville and Jacqueline Rogers. **Dell Books, a division of Bantam Doubleday Dell Publishing Group, Inc.,** for Peter Dickinson, "Unicorn," from *Merlin Dreams* by Peter Dickinson. Copyright ©1988 by Peter Dickinson. Illustration copyright ©1988 by Alan Lee. **Carol Kendall and Yao-wen Li,** for "Jade Soup," copyright ©1990 by Carol Kendall and Yao-wen Li. **William Morris Agency, Inc.,** for Leo Rosten, "Cemetery Path," Copyright ©1941, 1968 by Leo Rosten.

Copyright ©1996 by Globe Fearon Educational Publisher, a division of Simon & Schuster, 1 Lake Street, Upper Saddle River, New Jersey 07458. All rights reserved. No part of this book may be reproduced or transmitted in any form or by any means, electrical or mechanical, including photocopy-ing, recording, or by any information storage and retrieval system, without permission in writing from the publisher.

Printed in the United States of America
   3  4  5  6  7  8  9  10  99  98  97
ISBN: 0-8359-1369-4

**GLOBE FEARON EDUCATIONAL PUBLISHER**
**A Division of Simon & Schuster**
Upper Saddle River, New Jersey

# TABLE OF CONTENTS

# Making Choices

# READING STORIES WITH A TWIST

Life plays tricks on us when we least expect it. The strangest events may be waiting just around the corner. It doesn't always matter how well we plan our lives. Even the most carefully made plans can go wrong. Sometimes our worst mistakes can end up as blessings! The future is something that no one can predict.

All the *Stories with a Twist* have unexpected endings. They are journeys with surprise destinations. Some of them will make you laugh, but others are bound to frighten you. Some show what happens to vain, foolish, or dishonest people. Others reveal how the kindest and smartest people meet their fate or rise above it.

The book is divided into five units. The first is "Tricks of the Mind." Here are four stories that will make you shudder. Is it possible to scare yourself to death or to imagine that you are more than one person? You'll be surprised to learn what strange things the mind can do.

The next group of stories is "Lessons Learned." None of these lessons is sought out by the characters. They come unexpectedly. But in the end, the characters are better for having learned them. This is especially true of the young couple in O. Henry's "The Gift of the Magi." The lesson they learn is that love may be more valuable than any other gift one can give.

The third group of stories deals with "The Unexpected." Just when you think you know what's going to happen—wham!—everything gets turned upside-down. As you read these stories, try to guess how they'll end. Here's a hint: Expect to be surprised!

The fourth group of stories is called "Tempting Fate." Try to keep calm as you read what happens to people who try to fight destiny. When they tempt fate, they have to face the consequences. As you will see, when fate comes knocking at your door, you can run— but you can't hide!

What was the last tough decision that you had to make? Was it a matter of life and death? In the last unit, "Making Choices," people make decisions that are guaranteed to shock you. If you're brave enough, put yourself in their positions. What would you choose to do if you were in that position?

Sit in a comfortable chair when you read these stories. You'll be squirming in your seat with every twist and turn! Try to imagine the lives of the characters— when and where they lived and the motives behind their actions. Think about the plot, or series of the events, portrayed in each story. Ask yourself as you read: What is the conflict or struggle? How does it affect the final twist?

# Unit 1
## TRICKS OF THE MIND

# CEMETERY PATH

## Leo Rosten

*We all have fears. Think back to when you were a small child. Were you afraid of the dark? Did you insist that there were monsters hiding under your bed, or scary movie characters living in the closet?*

*Some people look at a cemetery and see a peaceful place of eternal rest. But to others, the mere thought of a cemetery gives them the creeps. They wouldn't dream of walking among the tombstones in the dark.*

*Ivan, the timid man in the story you are about to read, would never walk through the town cemetery to get to his home. Then, one fateful night, he agrees to do so on a bet. Perhaps Ivan should have followed his heart after all. For there in the cemetery, he encounters a terrible danger. But what is it? Read the story to find out.*

## VOCABULARY WORDS

**mocked** (MAHKT) made fun of
❖ The children *mocked* the little boy when he started to cry.

**taunts** (TAWNTS) remarks that cause anger
❖ After daily *taunts*, the child finally stood up to the bullies.

**jeered** (JIHRD) made rude remarks
❖ He *jeered* when the other team dropped the ball.

**quarry** (KWAHR-ee) anything being hunted or chased
❖ Our cat stalked its *quarry* and then pounced.

**saber** (SAY-buhr) a sword with a slightly curved blade
❖ The soldier drew his *saber* and urged his horse on.

**massive** (MAS-ihv) large and imposing
❖ They climbed to the top of the *massive* mountain.

**unyielding** (un-YEEL-dihng) not giving in to force
❖ This *unyielding* window will not open, no matter how hard I push.

**implacable** (ihm-PLAK-uh-buhl) not able to be eased or lessened
❖ The hurricane was an *implacable* force.

## KEY WORDS

**Ivan** (EYE-van) **the Terrible** the Russian czar who started a reign of terror in the 1500s
❖ In 1580, *Ivan the Terrible* killed his own son.

**Cossack** (KAHS-ak) a Russian horseman who served the czar
❖ The *Cossack* was feared by everyone in the village.

**rubles** (ROO-buhlz) unit of money used in Russia
❖ The man did not have enough *rubles* to buy a cow.

**I**van was a timid little man—so timid that the villagers called him "Pigeon" or mocked him with the title "Ivan the Terrible." Every night Ivan stopped in at the saloon which was on the edge of the village cemetery. Ivan never crossed the cemetery to get to his lonely shack on the other side. The path through the cemetery would save him many minutes, but he had never taken it—not even in the full light of noon.

Late one winter's night, when bitter wind and snow beat against the saloon, the customers took up the familiar mockery. "Ivan's mother was scared by a canary when she carried him in her womb." "Ivan the Terrible—Ivan the Terribly Timid One."

Ivan's sickly protest only fed their taunts, and they jeered cruelly when the young Cossack lieutenant flung his horrid challenge at their quarry.

"You are a pigeon, Ivan. You'll walk all around the cemetery in this fiendish cold—but you dare not cross the cemetery."

Ivan murmured, "The cemetery is nothing to cross, Lieutenant. It is nothing but earth, like all the other earth."

The lieutenant cried, "A challenge, then! Cross the cemetery tonight, Ivan, and I'll give you five rubles— five gold rubles!"

Perhaps it was the vodka. Perhaps it was the temptation of the five gold rubles. No one ever knew why Ivan, moistening his lips, said suddenly: "Yes, Lieutenant, I'll cross the cemetery!"

The saloon echoed with their disbelief. The lieutenant winked to the men and unbuckled his saber. "Here, Ivan. When you get to the center of the cemetery, in front of the biggest tomb, stick the saber into the ground. In the morning, we shall go there. And if the saber is in the ground—five gold rubles to you!"

Ivan took the saber. The men drank a toast: "To Ivan the Terrible!" They roared with laughter.

The wind howled around Ivan as he closed the door of the saloon behind him. The cold was knife-sharp. He buttoned his long coat and crossed the dirt road. He could hear the lieutenant's voice, louder than the rest, yelling after him, "Five rubles, pigeon! *If you live!*"

Ivan pushed the cemetery gate open. He walked fast. "Earth, just earth . . . like any other earth." But the darkness was a massive dread. "Five gold rubles . . ." The wind was cruel and the saber was like ice in his hands. Ivan shivered under the long, thick coat and broke into a limping run.

He recognized the large tomb. He must have sobbed—that was the sound that was drowned in the wind. And he kneeled, cold and terrified, and drove the saber into the hard ground. With his fist, he beat it down to the hilt. It was done. The cemetery . . . the challenge . . . five gold rubles.

Ivan started to rise from his knees. But he could not move. Something held him. Something gripped him in an unyielding and implacable hold. Ivan tugged and lurched and pulled—gasping in his panic, shaken by a monstrous fear. But something held Ivan. He cried out in terror, then made senseless gurgling noises.

They found Ivan, the next morning, on the ground in front of the tomb that was in the center of the cemetery. His face was not that of a frozen man's, but of a man killed by some nameless horror. And the lieutenant's saber was in the ground where Ivan had pounded it— through the dragging folds of his long coat.

## READING FOR UNDERSTANDING

**1.** How would you describe Ivan at the beginning of the story?

**2.** Why do you think the customers at the saloon called him "Ivan the Terrible"?

**3.** Why do you think the villagers treated Ivan the way they did?

**4.** What place did Ivan avoid?

**5.** What did the lieutenant promise to give Ivan if he would cross the cemetery?

**6.** Why do you think the lieutenant made the challenge?

**7.** Why did Ivan accept the lieutenant's challenge?

**8.** Why did Ivan stick the saber in the ground?

**9.** What was it that prevented Ivan from leaving the cemetery?

**10.** What do you think it was that really killed Ivan?

**11.** Had Ivan been right all along to avoid the cemetery? Why?

## RESPONDING TO THE STORY

Ivan is a person who is cruelly teased by everyone. Do you know someone who is always being teased? Imagine you are this person. Write a letter to an advice columnist, expressing how you feel. Then write a response to the letter.

## REVIEWING VOCABULARY

**1.** If the door is *unyielding*, then it **(a)** can't be opened **(b)** needs to be painted **(c)** needs to be locked.

**2.** Someone's *mockery* might make you **(a)** feel proud **(b)** say you're sorry **(c)** feel angry or sad.

**3.** When the new student heard the other students' *taunts*, he probably **(a)** felt happy **(b)** felt angry **(c)** said hello.

**4.** If a baseball player *jeered* at the catcher, he **(a)** made rude remarks **(b)** gave him a signal **(c)** praised his catching.

**5.** An example of a *quarry* is a cat **(a)** sleeping in the sun **(b)** drinking some milk **(c)** being chased by a dog.

**6.** A *saber* is used **(a)** in battle **(b)** to cut bread **(c)** to row.

**7.** A *massive* rock is **(a)** light **(b)** heavy **(c)** under water.

**8.** An *implacable* load **(a)** is easy to carry **(b)** can't be lessened **(c)** can't be found.

## THINKING CRITICALLY

**1.** A U.S. president once said: "The only thing we have to fear is fear itself." In your own words, explain what this means. How does the ending of this story prove it to be true?

**2.** Did Ivan have any real reasons to fear the cemetery? Do you think he should have avoided it just because he was afraid? Explain.

**3.** If Ivan had lived after crossing the cemetery, do you think that he would have been a changed man? Why or why not?

# THE BOY WHO DREW CATS

## adapted from a story by Lafcadio Hearn

*Do you ever think about living in another country? Lafcadio Hearn was an American who fell in love with Japan. He spent the last fifteen years of his life there. His stories combine the best of East and West. They tell about customs in Japan. They are also fun to read.*

*"The Boy Who Drew Cats" is a ghost story that sounds a little like a Japanese folk tale. It has a demon that even brave warriors cannot conquer. It has a fantastic event that happens inside a dusty Buddhist temple. But the main character of this story is very realistic. In fact, he may even remind you of some young graffiti artists of today.*

*It is this boy's skill as an artist that lands him in a heap of trouble. Yet even the worst kind of trouble can't prevent him from drawing his favorite subject—cats. He draws cats everywhere: on paper or on walls. It doesn't matter where. Then one day, this habit of his comes in handy. Read this story with a surprising twist to find out how.*

## VOCABULARY WORDS

**acolyte** (AK-uh-lyt) helper, attendant
❖ The priest agreed to train the boy as an *acolyte* and to put him to work at the temple.

**obedient** (oh-BEE-dee-uhnt) willing to obey
❖ The little girl was so *obedient* that her teacher gave her a special award.

**pillars** (PIHL-uhrs) columns used to hold up a building
❖ The heavy tile roof was supported by eighteen *pillars*.

**sorrowfully** (SAHR-oh-fuhl-lee) with feelings of sadness
❖ After the funeral, they went home *sorrowfully*.

**goblin** (GOB-lihn) evil spirit
❖ Because a fierce *goblin* was haunting the temple, all the priests left and the building was closed up.

**principal** (PRIHN-suh-puhl) main, chief
❖ The large shops were all on the *principal* avenue, not on the side streets.

**chink** (CHIHNK) narrow opening, slit
❖ The boy watched the street through a *chink* in the window curtain.

 **A long time ago,** in a small country village in Japan, there lived a poor farmer and his wife. They were very good people. They had a number of children and found it very hard to feed them all. When he was only fourteen years old, their oldest son was strong enough to help his father. The little girls learned to help their mother almost as soon as they could walk.

But the youngest, a little boy, did not seem to be suited for hard work. He was very clever—more clever than all his brothers and sisters. But he was quite weak and small, and people said he would never grow to be very big. So his parents thought it would be better for him to become a priest rather than a farmer. They took him with them to the village temple one day. They asked the good old priest who lived there if he would make their little boy his acolyte, and teach him all that a priest ought to know.

The old priest spoke kindly to the boy and asked him some difficult questions. So clever were the answers that the priest agreed to take the little fellow on as an acolyte, and to educate him for the priest-hood.

The boy learned quickly what the old priest taught him, and was obedient in most things. But he had one fault. He liked to draw cats during study hour. He even drew cats where he was not supposed to draw them.

Whenever he found himself alone, he drew cats. He drew them on the margins of the old priest's books, and on the screens of the temple, and on the walls, and on the pillars. Several times, the priest told him to stop. But he did not stop drawing cats. He drew them because he could not really help it. He had what is called "the genius of an artist," and just for that reason

**11**

the priest felt that he was not well suited to be an acolyte. A good acolyte should study books.

One day, after he had drawn some very clever pictures of cats upon a paper screen, the old priest said to him severely, "My boy, you must go away from this temple at once. You will never make a good priest, but perhaps you will become a great artist. Now, let me give you a last piece of advice, and be sure you never forget it. *Avoid large places at night—keep to small!*"

The boy did not know what the priest meant by saying, *"Avoid large places—keep to small!"* He thought and thought while he was tying up his little bundle of clothes to take with him. But he could not understand the old priest's advice. And he was afraid to speak to the priest any more, except to say good-bye.

He left the temple very sorrowfully and began to wonder what he should do. If he went straight home, he felt sure his father would punish him for having been disobedient to the old priest. So he was afraid to go home. All at once he remembered that in the next village, twelve miles away, there was a very big temple. He had heard there were several priests at that temple. He made up his mind to go to them and ask them to take him on as their acolyte.

Now, that big temple had been closed up, but the boy did not know this fact. The reason that it had been closed up was that a goblin had frightened the priests away and had taken over the place. Afterward, some brave warriors had gone to the temple at night, but they had never been seen alive again. Nobody had ever told these things to the boy, so he walked all the way to the village, expecting to be treated kindly by the priests.

When he got to the village, it was already dark and all the people were in bed. He saw the big temple on a hill at the other end of the principal street, and he saw that there was a light in the temple. People who tell the story say that the goblin used to make that light in order to attract lonely travelers seeking shelter for the night.

The boy went at once to the temple and knocked on the main door. There was no sound inside. He knocked and knocked again, but still nobody came. At last, he pushed gently at the door and was quite glad to find that it was not locked. So he went in and saw a lamp burning—but no priest.

He thought that a priest would be sure to come very soon, and he sat down and waited. Then he noticed that everything in the temple was gray with dust and thickly spun over with cobwebs. So he thought to himself that the priests would certainly like to have an acolyte to clean the temple. He wondered why they had allowed everything to get so dusty. What most pleased him, however, were some big white screens that were good to paint cats upon. Though he was tired, he ground some ink and began at once to paint cats.

He painted a great many cats upon the screens. Then he began to feel very, very sleepy. He was just on the point of lying down to sleep beside one of the screens when he suddenly remembered the old priest's advice: *"Avoid large places—keep to small!"*

The temple was very large, and he was all alone. As he thought of these words—though he could not quite understand them—he began to feel a little afraid for the first time. He decided to look for a small place in which to sleep. He found a little cabinet with a sliding door, slid it open, got in, and slid the door closed. Then he lay down and fell fast asleep.

Very late in the night, he was awakened by a most terrible noise—a noise of fighting and screaming. It was so dreadful that he was afraid even to look through a chink in the little cabinet. He lay very still, holding his breath in fright.

The light that had been in the temple went out, but the awful sounds continued. They became more awful, and all the temple shook. After a long time, silence came, but the boy was still afraid to move. He did not move until the light of the morning sun shone into the cabinet through the chinks in the door.

He then got out of his hiding place very cautiously and looked about. The first thing he saw was that the floor of the temple was covered with blood. And then he saw, lying dead in the middle of it, an enormous, monstrous rat—a goblin-rat—bigger than a cow!

But who or what could have killed it? There was no man or other creature to be seen. Suddenly, the boy

noticed that all the mouths of the cats he had drawn
the night before were red and wet with blood. Then he
knew that the cats he had drawn had killed the goblins.
And then also, for the first time, he understood why the
wise old priest had said to him: *"Avoid large places at
night—keep to small."*

Afterward, the boy became a very famous artist.
Some of the cats which he drew are still shown to travelers in Japan.

## READING FOR UNDERSTANDING

**1.** Arrange the following incidents in the order in which they occurred:

   **(a)** The boy saw the dead goblin-rat.
   **(b)** The old priest sent the boy away.
   **(c)** The old priest questioned the boy.
   **(d)** The boy became a famous artist.
   **(e)** The boy hid himself in a small cabinet.
   **(f)** The boy drew cats all over the books and walls.

**2.** Why did the boy's parents take him to the old priest?

**3.** According to the author, why couldn't the boy stop drawing cats?

**4.** Why did the boy go to another temple instead of going home to his family?

**5.** Why was the big temple all closed up?

**6.** What saved the boy from being killed by the enormous goblin-rat?

**7.** What do you think the priest meant by saying, *"Avoid large places at night—stick to small"*?

## RESPONDING TO THE STORY

This story tells what happens to a boy who has such great artistic talent that he cannot stop himself from drawing. Would you like to be this character? In a paragraph, explain why or why not.

## REVIEWING VOCABULARY

Match each word on the left with the correct definition
on the right.

| | | | |
|---|---|---|---|
| **1.** acolyte | **a.** narrow opening |
| **2.** goblin | **b.** main |
| **3.** sorrowfully | **c.** evil spirit |
| **4.** principal | **d.** willing to obey |
| **5.** chink | **e.** helper |
| **6.** obedient | **f.** columns |
| **7.** pillars | **g.** with feelings of sadness |

## THINKING CRITICALLY

**1.** Do you think the priest was right to make the boy
leave the temple? Explain your answer in a paragraph.
**2.** What is the mood or tone of the story? Did you
enjoy reading it? Why? Why not? How do you
think the story's tone affected your reading?
Support your answer with examples from the story.
**3.** In this story, the goblin takes the form of a large
rat. What do you think would have happened if the
goblin had been a giant dog? Would there have
been a different ending to the story?

# THE WAKE-UP CALL

## Roberta Simpson Brown

*Nancy Logan takes a job as a desk clerk at a hotel, despite a funny feeling that she shouldn't. She really needs the money, and it does appear to be just an ordinary job. But from the very first moment, something seems wrong.*

*Have you ever had a strange feeling that something terrible will happen? For example, did you ever get into a car and, for no reason, feel that you were riding toward danger? Did that feeling ever turn out to be true? Do you believe in "gut" feelings about the future? Can they really foretell the dangers that may lie ahead?*

*Be ready for a chilling ending when you read this story. It's a ghost story that will leave you shuddering with horror.*

## VOCABULARY WORDS

**indistinctly** (ihn-dihs-TIHNGKT-lee) in a way that is not clear to the eye, ear, or mind
❖ The old woman spoke *indistinctly*, so I asked her to repeat her name.

**disgruntled** (dihs-GRUN-tuhld) discontented
❖ The *disgruntled* woman asked us to refund her money.

**surged** (SERJD) rushed strongly
❖ The wave *surged* over the dock.

**incompetent** (ihn-KAHM-puh-tuhnt) not able to do a job or task well
❖ The *incompetent* worker was fired from his job.

**renovated** (REHN-uh-vay-tuhd) fixed to a good or new condition
❖ The *renovated* store is much nicer and attracts more customers.

**conceded** (kuhn-SEED-uhd) admitted as true
❖ When all the votes were counted, he *conceded* that he had lost the election.

**throb** (THRAHB) beat strongly
❖ As the player caught the ball, my heart began to *throb*.

**whiff** (WHIHF) a slight gust of air or smoke or odor
❖ I got a *whiff* of fresh-baked bread.

**charred** (CHAHRD) blackened due to burning
❖ After the fire, they found only the *charred* remains of their cabin.

**N**ancy Logan had never had a premonition of danger before the day she accepted the job to replace the missing desk clerk at the Grand Rockport Hotel. As she straightened her skirt and waited at the front desk to greet the first guest, she still felt like she shouldn't be here. But her bank balance told her otherwise, so she checked in the first guest, handed him the key, and rang for the bellhop.

The guest took the key and followed the bellhop to the elevator. Nancy relaxed as she watched. This job might not be so tough, after all.

Nancy looked at her list of things to do. She should probably make sure that the wake-up calls were made first. The night clerk had checked off all except 321. It was due now. She picked up the phone.

A tapping on the desk interrupted her. A little gray-haired lady was staring at her impatiently. Nancy hadn't seen her come in, and she had no idea of how long she had been standing there. It couldn't have been long. It had only taken her a minute to check her list. She decided she'd better make the wake-up call before she got involved with the lady.

"I'll be with you in a minute, ma'am," said Nancy. She gave the lady a bright smile while she punched the numbers.

"I don't have all day!" the lady snapped.

Nancy could hear the phone ringing as she watched the old woman drumming her fingers on the desk.

"That's been ringing long enough to wake the dead," said the woman. "Nobody's going to answer."

Nancy was about to agree and hang up, when someone picked up the receiver. A man's voice spoke, but Nancy couldn't understand what he was saying. He

**20**

coughed and wheezed between words. Other voices were speaking indistinctly in the background.

"Good morning, sir," said Nancy. "I have a seven o'clock wake-up call for 321. Is everything all right, sir?"

"Ep," the man mumbled. "Room 213."

Nancy was confused. His reply sounded more like "help" than "yep." But if he were ill, surely the other people in the room must be helping him. Had he said Room 213? She was almost positive that he had. If so, she had dialed the wrong number, but she didn't think she had. She'd been very careful.

She started to ask again if she had the right room and if he was all right, but a loud, crackling sound began on the line and she was cut off.

Nancy stood debating whether or not to hang up and try again, but the little old woman at the desk decided for her.

"Are you going to help me, young lady," she asked, "or do I call the manager?"

Nancy hung up the phone.

"I'm sorry, ma'am," she told the lady.

She checked the old woman in, rang for assistance with the luggage, and let out a breath of relief as she watched the disgruntled guest cross the lobby.

Her relief was short-lived.

The phone rang and Nancy picked it up. A man's angry voice surged through the line.

"This is Mr. Carson in 321. What kind of incompetent hotel are you running? I asked for a wake-up call at seven sharp. It's now 7:17! It's lucky I woke up. I'm going to be late as it is!"

He slammed the phone down before Nancy could explain her mistake. He would have still been angry, even with an explanation. Nancy didn't blame him.

How could she have mixed up those numbers? The man she'd reached earlier really had said 213! The old woman must have distracted her. Now she'd have to apologize to the man in 213 and to Mr. Carson in 321.

She checked to see who was registered in 213, but she could find no one listed.

Perhaps she'd better explain the whole thing to her supervisor before she made any apologies. She buzzed his office, hoping he'd understand.

"Mr. Hart," she began when he answered, "I've made my first mistake of the day already."

He listened while she explained the mix-up. When he spoke, his voice sounded odd instead of angry.

"Nancy, you couldn't have reached 213. That room is part of the suite that was destroyed by the fire last year. We renovated it, but we got so many complaints from guests, we closed it permanently and disconnected the phone."

"I'm sure the man said 213," Nancy insisted.

"You must have misunderstood," he told her, "or the man must have been mistaken about what room he was in."

"Maybe," Nancy conceded reluctantly. In her own mind, she still wasn't convinced.

"Trust me," said Mr. Hart. "Nobody has spent an entire night there since the fire. The guests say they can't sleep, and they insist on being moved to another room."

"Why?" asked Nancy.

"I guess you don't know," he said. "I keep forgetting that you are new in town. A family of four died in that fire."

"No, I hadn't heard about it," said Nancy.

"It was a terrible thing," Mr. Hart continued. "They were asleep. The desk clerk had forgotten to make the wake-up call. He just dropped out of sight after that. I guess he felt that he was responsible."

"Was he the one I replaced?" asked Nancy.

"Yes," replied Mr. Hart. "After he left, a lot of wild stories started going around about 213."

"What kind of stories?" asked Nancy.

"Oh, you know," said Mr. Hart. "The horror tales you'd expect. People that stayed in that room after the fire claimed they heard coughing and wheezing and voices asking for help."

"But that's what I heard when I called!" said Nancy. "Were there any other stories?"

"One guest claimed he saw the desk clerk that used to work here. You know, that kind of nonsense."

"Do you think someone could have sneaked in and could actually be staying up there?" she asked.

"We only use it for storage now," he told her. "People seem to let their imaginations run wild when something like this happens. Just apologize to Mr. Carson and forget it. As you said, it was only a mistake."

Nancy hung up and dialed 321. Mr. Carson didn't answer. She'd try to catch him later and apologize face to face. That would probably be more effective.

She stood there a minute, wondering what would happen if she dialed 213. She decided to try it. She touched the numbers and listened to the ringing on the other end. Someone picked up the receiver again, but the crackling started immediately.

Nancy slammed the receiver down. She had been right! Somebody had answered in that room! Her head began to throb and without knowing why, she reached for a pad and pen and began scribbling. She was surprised to see what she had written: *Wake-up call. Seven o'clock. Room 213.* It didn't even look like her handwriting! The throbbing in her head stopped as suddenly as it had started. She shuddered and tossed the pad on top of some papers in a tray on the desk. Nothing like that had ever happened to her before.

Something odd was going on in this hotel! She was sure that somebody was in that room. She was getting more and more curious about who it could be, and remembered she had a break coming. It surely wouldn't hurt to take a look. The key marked 213 was there, so she took it and hurried to the elevator.

Nobody was in the hall near the door. She was glad of that, for she didn't want anybody to see her. She stood outside 213 and listened for a moment, but she heard nothing. She got a whiff of stale smoke as she bent over to unlock the door. She hesitated. Maybe she ought to forget this. Mr. Hart might not like it if he found out that she had been poking around up here. And she had to admit, she was a little frightened after hearing his stories.

She couldn't stand by the door all day. She had to do something. She compromised. She would open the door and just peek in from the hall.

Turning the knob and pulling the door open was her second mistake of the day.

A blast of hot air sucked her to the center of the room. Flames were all around her, devouring the curtains and carpet. Smoke ate away at her eyes and throat, and she began to cough.

The hotel was on fire! She had to get help! She tried to reach the door, but a wall of heat pushed her back.

A chorus of groans came from behind her, and she turned to see who it was. From the beds rose four black figures, rubbing chunks of charred flesh from their cheeks as they sleepily opened their empty eyes.

A ghostly figure in a desk clerk's uniform crouched

in terror near the phone, gasping over and over, "Wake-up call! Wake-up call!"

The smoke and the smell of burning flesh overcame Nancy, and she fell to the floor. The fire crept up slowly at first. Then it leapt on her hungrily, until she was covered by flames.

Mr. Hart wondered why Nancy didn't return from her break. He had waited a while before hiring someone after the fire because he wanted someone dependable. He had thought Nancy was just that. She seemed like such a sensible girl. He must have scared her off with his stories.

Business had picked up, so he had to hire a replacement for Nancy. He hoped this one would be more reliable! He explained the desk clerk's duties to her, and then went into his office.

The new girl reached in the tray for a pad to list the things he'd told her to do. She read the note that Nancy had scribbled. Her head began to throb. She wanted to make a good impression. She wrote down the wake-up call as the very first item on her day's agenda.

## READING FOR UNDERSTANDING

1. We could assume at the beginning of the story that something bad will happen because **(a)** Nancy knew the missing clerk **(b)** Nancy felt that she shouldn't have been working at the hotel **(c)** Nancy liked to greet guests.
2. Nancy took the job because she **(a)** needed the money **(b)** knew everyone who worked there **(c)** had nothing better to do.
3. Nancy found out that room 213 was registered to **(a)** Mr. Carson **(b)** the old woman **(c)** no one.
4. After Nancy talked to Mr. Hart, she **(a)** was glad that no one was in 213 **(b)** felt that Mr. Hart had lied to her **(c)** wanted to prove to herself that someone really was in 213.
5. Nancy didn't want anyone to see her enter 213 because **(a)** she was on her break **(b)** she knew she was snooping and didn't want Mr. Hart to find out **(c)** she planned to stay there.
6. We can assume that the new desk clerk will **(a)** quit after one day **(b)** have an experience very similar to Nancy's **(c)** save the people in 213.

## RESPONDING TO THE STORY

A premonition is a feeling that something bad will happen. Nancy had a premonition of danger about her new job at the hotel. She began it anyway. Tell about a time when you or someone you know had a premonition that something would go wrong. Write a paragraph describing what happened.

## REVIEWING VOCABULARY

The following sentences are based on the story. Decide which of the words following the sentences best fits each blank. Write your answers on a separate sheet of paper.

**1.** Nancy heard other voices _____ in the background.

**2.** The little old woman at the desk became very _____.

**3.** The angry voice _____ through the phone lines.

**4.** Mr. Carson said that they ran an _____ hotel.

**5.** After 213 was destroyed by the fire, they _____ it.

**6.** Nancy _____ that she might have misunderstood the man who answered the wake-up call.

**7.** When Nancy unlocked 213, she got a _____ of stale smoke.

**8.** Four figures rubbed _____ flesh from their cheeks.

**9.** The confusion began to make her head _____.

**Words:** *charred, conceded, disgruntled, incompetent, throb, indistinctly, renovated, surged, whiff*

## THINKING CRITICALLY

**1.** How does the author create suspense in this story? Describe the sequence of events that helps increase the tension.

**2.** Think about the ending of this story. What would you change to make the ending sound realistic? What did Nancy really find in room 213?

# WILLIAM WILSON

## adapted from a story by Edgar Allan Poe

*The central character in this story by Edgar Allan Poe is followed all over the world by a mysterious figure. Each time the character tries to do something wrong, he is stopped by this mysterious person. But who, exactly, could it be? Perhaps it is his conscience, or sense of right and wrong, come to life.*

*Have you ever felt that your conscience was like a person following you? If you could stare your conscience straight in the face, what would it look like? In this chilling story by Poe, the face of the main character's conscience is just too much for him to bear.*

*Many of Poe's stories deal with dark and hidden fears. As you read "William Wilson," see if you can predict its bizarre and surprising ending.*

# VOCABULARY WORDS

**namesake** (NAYM-sayk) person with the same name as another
❖ Aunt Laura is my *namesake*.

**hostility** (hahs-TIHL-uh-tee) ill will
❖ Their frowns showed their *hostility*.

**contempt** (cuhn-TEHMPT) feeling of dislike
❖ I was filled with *contempt* toward the liar.

**sarcastic** (sahr-KAS-tihk) mocking or bitterness intended to insult
❖ Her *sarcastic* tone of voice angered me.

**composure** (kuhm-POH-zhuhr) calmness of mind or manner
❖ Nothing could disturb her *composure*.

**destiny** (DEHS-tuh-nee) things that happen in one's life that are believed to be predetermined
❖ His *destiny* was to become a rich man.

**masquerade** (mas-kuh-RAYD) party at which masks are worn
❖ We went to a *masquerade* on Halloween.

**scoundrel** (SKOWN-druhl) an evil person
❖ The man who stole your bicycle was a *scoundrel*.

# KEY WORDS

**Oxford** (AHKS-fuhrd) famous university in England
❖ Many leaders of Great Britain attended *Oxford*.

**écarté** (ay-kahr-TAY) card game
❖ In France and England during the last century, *écarté* was a popular card game.

 **L**et me call myself **William Wilson.** The page upon which I now write need not reveal my real name. Death approaches, and I long, in passing, for the sympathy of my fellow men.

My earliest memories of school life are connected with a large, rambling house in a village in England. There were a vast number of gigantic trees, and all the houses in the village were very old. I passed the years of my life between ten and fifteen surrounded by the huge walls of the school. My energy, enthusiasm, and strong personality soon made me a special person among my friends. By slow but natural steps, I gained power over nearly all of them—with one exception.

This was a student who, although no relation, had the same name as myself. My namesake alone, of those who were in our group, competed with me in class and on the playground. He refused either to believe that I was special or to submit to my will.

Wilson's rebellion embarrassed me. In spite of how I treated him in public, I secretly feared him. I could not help thinking that the fairness with which he treated me was proof of his true superiority. Not to be beaten by him cost me a constant struggle. Yet his superiority—even his fairness—was in truth seen by no one but myself. Our friends, by some strange blindness, seemed not even to suspect it.

I casually learned that my namesake was born on the 19th of January, 1813. By an amazing coincidence, it is precisely the day of my own birth.

It may seem strange that in spite of my constant fear of Wilson, I could not bring myself to hate him. It is difficult, indeed, to define, or even to describe, my real feelings toward him. They formed a mixture—

some anger, which was not yet hatred, some esteem, more respect, much fear, with a world of uneasy curiosity.

It was no doubt the odd state of affairs existing between us which turned all my attacks upon him into practical jokes. In this way, I avoided more serious actions. My rival had a weak throat, which prevented him from raising his voice at any time above a very low whisper. I did not fail to take advantage of this weak voice by mocking it.

Wilson made attacks on me. There was one form of his practical wit that disturbed me more than the others. It was the way he imitated me in dress and manner. Even my voice did not escape him. No one seemed to notice this mockery of me. Even so, I found it unbearable.

One night near the end of my fifth year at school, I arose from bed and stole to the bedroom of my rival. I took a light and with it approached his bed.

The bright rays fell vividly upon the sleeper. I looked at his face. My whole body was instantly filled with a feeling of coldness and numbness. My chest heaved. My knees tottered. Gasping for breath, I lowered the lamp still nearer to the face. The same name! The same day of birth! And now, even when asleep, the same face as my own!

Had his mockery of my voice and manner been stamped into his features forever? I had not expected him to look like me even when asleep. I pulled away the lamp and left the chamber silently. I left that school the next day, never to return to it again.

Many years later, when I was at Oxford, there came to the university a rich but dumb young nobleman, Glendenning. I frequently played cards with him, allowing him to win large sums, in order to trap him.

Then I took the next step in my plan to make a fool of him. I met him in the rooms of my friend Preston. I had arranged to have a party of some eight or ten present. I was very careful that the introduction of cards should appear accidental.

We had sat up far into the night. I had finally got Glendenning alone at my favorite card game, écarté. The rest of the group had left their own cards and were looking on. Glendenning, who had earlier drunk too much, now shuffled, dealt, or played with a wild nervousness. In a very short period, he owed me a great deal of money. Then, he did precisely what I had been coolly waiting for. He proposed to double our already large stakes. I pretended to be reluctant, then finally agreed. The result, of course, proved how entirely he was in my power. In less than an hour, he had bet four times as much. I had thought him very wealthy. But when I won by my cheating, his utter cry of despair filled the room. I realized I had caused his total ruin.

The sad condition of Glendenning had thrown an air of embarrassed gloom over all. For some moments, a deep silence fell. I could not help feeling my cheeks tingle. Then the heavy folding doors of the apartment were suddenly thrown open. The rush of air blew out all the candles in the room. Their light, in dying, allowed us just to see that a stranger, about my own height and wrapped in a cloak, had entered. Before any of us could recover, we heard the voice of the intruder.

"Gentlemen," he said, in a low, distinct, and thrilling whisper. "Gentlemen, I make no apology for this behavior. I am but doing a duty. You are, beyond doubt, unaware of the true character of this William Wilson. He has just won a large sum of money from Lord Glendenning. I will therefore suggest to you a plan for finding out how he really won it. Please examine the inner linings of the cuff of his left sleeve, and the several little packages which may be found in the pockets of his cloak."

While he spoke, the room was still. One could have heard a pin drop. When he finished, he left as abruptly as he had come. Can I—shall I describe my feeling? Must I say that I felt all the horrors of the damned? But I had little time for thought. Many hands roughly seized me, and lights were quickly brought. A search followed. In the lining of my sleeve were found all the court cards needed in écarté, and, in my pockets, a number of packs, copies of those used at our games. Everything I had used in my plan of deception was now revealed.

There was no burst of hostility upon this discovery. Only silent contempt for me filled the room. Everyone looked at me with sarcastic composure.

"Mr. Wilson," said our host, "you will see the necessity, I hope, of leaving Oxford, and of leaving my room now."

I left, but I couldn't stop thinking about one horrifying detail of what had just happened. The coat I was wearing was made of rare fur. It was extremely costly. Wilson had been wearing one exactly like it!

I fled in vain. My evil destiny pursued me as if in joy. It proved, indeed, that the exercise of its mysterious power had as yet only begun. Scarcely had I set foot in Paris before I had fresh evidence of the hateful interest taken by this Wilson in my concerns. Years flew by, while I had no relief. Villain! At Rome, he stepped in between me and my plans! At Vienna, too—at Berlin—and at Moscow! In every place I went, I discovered a better reason to curse him within my heart. Could he, for an instant, have supposed that I had failed to recognize my biggest enemy and evil genius, the William Wilson of my schoolboy days? Impossible!—But let me go on to the last big scene of the drama.

It was at Rome, during the Carnival of 18—, that I attended a masquerade at the palace of the Duke Di Broglio. I had drunk more wine than usual. Now the close atmosphere of the crowded rooms was more than I could bear. The difficulty, too, of forcing my way through the crowd annoyed me. I was eagerly seeking the young, the gay, the beautiful wife of the aging Di Broglio. She had already told me what costume she would be wearing. Now, having caught sight of her, I was hurrying to make my way to her. Suddenly, I felt a light hand placed upon my shoulder, and I heard that familiar, low whisper in my ear.

In an absolute rage, I turned at once upon him who had stopped me, and seized him violently by the collar. He was dressed in a costume similar to my own. He was wearing a Spanish cloak of blue velvet with a crimson belt about the waist holding a dagger. A mask of black silk covered his face.

"Scoundrel!" I exclaimed, in a husky voice while every word I spoke seemed to add fuel to my fury. "Scoundrel! Impostor! Evil villain! You shall not—*you shall not*—dog me unto death! Follow me, or I will stab you where you stand!" And I made my way from the ballroom into the small chamber next door, pulling him along with me as I went.

Upon entering, I thrust him furiously from me. He fell against the wall, while I closed the door. I ordered him to draw his weapon. He hesitated only for an instant. Then, with a slight sigh, he prepared to defend himself.

The contest was brief indeed. In a few seconds, I forced him by sheer strength against the wall panels.

Getting him at mercy, I plunged my sword, with brute fury, again and again through his chest.

At that instant, some person tried to open the door. I rushed to prevent an intrusion. I immediately returned to my dying opponent. But what human language can fully express my astonishment and horror at the sight before me? During the brief moment in which I had turned away, the room had changed. A large mirror—so at first it seemed to me in my confusion—now stood where none had been before. As I stepped up to it in an agony of terror, my own image came forward to meet me with a halting step. But the features were all pale and bloody.

Thus it seemed, I say, but was not. It was my opponent—it was Wilson, who then stood before me. His mask and cloak lay, where he had thrown them, on the floor. There was not a thread in all his clothing—not a line in all the features of his face which was not, even in the smallest detail, my own!

It was Wilson. But he spoke no longer in a whisper, and I could have believed that I myself was speaking while he said:

"You have won, and I give up. Yet, from this moment on, you are also dead—dead to the world, to Heaven, and to hope! In me did you exist—and, in my death, see by this image, which is your own, how utterly you have murdered yourself!"

# READING FOR UNDERSTANDING

1. This story is mainly about the conflict between William Wilson and **(a)** his classmate **(b)** his namesake **(c)** his conscience, or sense of right and wrong.

2. Most of the story takes place in **(a)** Rome **(b)** Paris **(c)** England.

3. The narrator first met his namesake when he was **(a)** a boy at school **(b)** a university student at Oxford **(c)** on a ship to America.

4. When he was at Oxford, the narrator tried to cheat Lord Glendenning **(a)** in a land deal **(b)** at cards **(c)** on a bet about a football match.

5. At the masquerade, William Wilson and his namesake wore **(a)** similar costumes **(b)** feather masks **(c)** different costumes.

6. Wilson challenged his namesake to a fight in hopes of **(a)** keeping him away from the Duke's wife **(b)** winning him over as a friend **(c)** killing him.

7. We can assume that the narrator began to hate his rival because he **(a)** never spoke above a whisper **(b)** was liked by the Duchess **(c)** followed him everywhere like a conscience.

8. Wilson's final speech showed that he **(a)** did not really die **(b)** forgave the narrator **(c)** and his namesake were the same person.

# RESPONDING TO THE STORY

When we hurt other people, it is ourselves that we hurt most of all. How does the story suggest this? Discuss your responses with a small group of classmates.

## REVIEWING VOCABULARY

The sentences below are based on the story. Decide which of the words following the sentences best fits each blank. Write your answers on a separate sheet of paper.

1. Wilson hid his _____ toward his namesake by playing jokes on him.
2. After the card game, everyone looked at Wilson with _____.
3. William Wilson feels that he is being chased by some evil _____.
4. The end of the story takes place at a _____ party where everyone wears masks.
5. After he was found to be a cheat, the narrator could not keep his _____.

**Words:** *contempt, hostility, destiny, composure, masquerade*

## THINKING CRITICALLY

1. In most of the story, William Wilson's namesake never speaks above a low whisper. But just before he dies, he does. His last speech is said to be "no longer in a whisper." Why do you think the author made this change?
2. Wilson is filled with opposing feelings about his namesake. In some ways he detests him. What other feelings does he have? Why do you think his feelings shift?
3. Do you think Poe's portrayal of Wilson's conscience is effective? Why or why not? Give examples to support your response.

# Unit 2
## LESSONS LEARNED

# THE GIFT OF THE MAGI

## adapted from a story by O. Henry

*How far would you go to buy a present for someone you love? Would you sell your most prized possession to get the money to pay for it? If you would, you will like the two characters in the story you are about to read. They are so much in love with each other that they are willing to make great sacrifices for each other.*

*"The Gift of the Magi" is one of O. Henry's most famous stories. It speaks to everyone who has ever wanted to buy a gift that he or she couldn't afford. It also shows in a sad but amusing way that even our best intentions don't always turn out as we expected.*

*Though "The Gift of the Magi" takes place one hundred years ago in New York City, it is not restricted to that time or place. After all, it is a love story, and love stories are timeless.*

## VOCABULARY WORDS

**predominating** (pree-DAHM-uh-nayt-ihng) prevailing, happening most often
❖ Anger was the *predominating* mood in the election.

**cascade** (kas-KAYD) a small, steep waterfall
❖ When she let her hair down, it was like a *cascade*.

**ransacking** (RAN-sak-ihng) searching well
❖ I was *ransacking* the stores for a gift.

**platinum** (PLAT-ihn-uhm) a precious metal, silvery in color
❖ Many people consider *platinum* more precious than gold.

**fob** (FAHB) **chain** chain for a pocket watch
❖ Grandpa wore his watch with a handsome *fob chain*.

**prudence** (PROOD-uhns) careful and sound judgment
❖ We begged him to show *prudence* in driving the car.

**craved** (KRAYVD) longed for eagerly
❖ After months of hard work, they *craved* a holiday.

## KEY WORDS

**Queen of Sheba** (SHEE-buh) the Arabian queen who visited King Solomon to test his wisdom
❖ The ancient land of *Sheba* lay in the Middle East.

**King Solomon** (SAHL-uh-muhn) Biblical king of Israel
❖ The reign of *Solomon* was mostly peaceful.

**Magi** (MAY-jeye) the three wise men who brought gifts to the Babe in the manger.
❖ In the story of the *Magi*, the three wise men followed a star to Bethlehem, where they found the infant Jesus.

**O**ne dollar and eighty-seven cents.
That was all. And sixty cents of it was in
pennies. Pennies saved, one and two at a
time, by arguing with the grocer and the
vegetable man and the butcher until one's
cheeks burned from penny-pinching. Della counted it
three times. One dollar and eighty-seven cents. And the
next day would be Christmas.

There was clearly nothing to do but flop down on
the shabby little couch and cry. Della did so, thinking
quite seriously that life is made up of sobs, sniffles, and
smiles, with sniffles predominating.

Della finished her cry and wiped her cheeks. She
stood by the window and looked out dully—without
expression—at a gray cat walking a gray fence in a
gray backyard. Tomorrow would be Christmas Day, and
she had only $1.87 with which to buy Jim a present.
She had been saving every penny she could for months,
but twenty dollars a week doesn't go far. Expenses had
been greater than she had planned. They always were.
Only $1.87 to buy a present for Jim. Her Jim. Many a
happy hour she had spent planning for something nice
for him. She wanted something fine and rare—something just a little bit near to being worthy of the honor
of being married to Jim.

Suddenly, she whirled from the window and stood
before the mirror. Her eyes were shining brilliantly, but
her face had lost its color within twenty seconds.
Rapidly she pulled down her hair and let it fall to its
full length.

Now, the James Dillingham Youngs had two possessions in which they both took a mighty pride. One was
Jim's gold watch that had been his father's and his
grandfather's. The other was Della's hair. If the Queen

of Sheba had lived in the apartment across the airshaft, Della would have let her hair hang out the window some day to dry just to make fun of Her Majesty's jewels and gifts. If King Solomon had been the janitor, with all his treasures piled up in the basement, Jim would have pulled out his watch every time the king passed, just to see him pull at his beard with envy.

Della's beautiful hair fell about her, rippling and shining like a cascade of brown waters. It reached below her knees and made itself almost a garment for her. And then, she did it up again nervously and quickly. She hesitated for a minute and stood still while a tear or two splashed on the worn red carpet.

On went her old brown jacket. On went her old brown hat. With a whirl of skirts and with the brilliant sparkle still in her eyes, she fluttered out the door and down the stairs to the street.

After rushing several blocks, she stopped suddenly. A sign on the building read: "Madame Sofronie. Hair Goods of All Kinds." Della entered and ran up a flight of stairs. Out of breath, she knocked on the door. She stood, still panting, before Madame Sofronie.

"Will you buy my hair?" asked Della.

"I buy hair," said Madame. "Take yer hat off, and let's have a sight at the looks of it."

Down rippled the brown cascade.

"Twenty dollars," said Madame, lifting the mass with a practiced hand.

"Give it to me quick," said Della.

The next two hours tripped by on rosy wings. Della was ransacking the stores for Jim's present.

She found it at last. It surely had been made for Jim and no one else. There was none other like it in any of the stores, and she had turned all of them inside out. It was a platinum fob chain, simple in design, properly proclaiming its value by substance alone and not by fancy decoration—as all good things should do. It was even worthy of The Watch. As soon as she saw it, she knew that it was meant to be Jim's. It was just like him. Quietness and value—the description applied to both. Twenty-one dollars she paid for it, and she hurried home with the 87 cents.

When Della reached home, her joy gave way a little to prudence and reason. She got out her curling irons and lighted the gas and went to work repairing the damage done by generosity added to love. Which is always a tremendous task, dear friends—a huge task.

Within forty seconds, her head was covered with tiny, close-lying curls that made her look wonderfully like a delinquent schoolboy. She looked at her reflection in the mirror, carefully and critically.

"If Jim doesn't kill me," she said to herself, "before he takes a second look at me, he'll say I look like a Coney Island chorus girl. But what could I do—oh, what could I do with a dollar and eighty-seven cents?"

At 7 o'clock, the coffee was made and the frying pan was on the back of the stove, hot and ready to cook the chops.

Jim was never late. Della doubled the fob chain in her hand and sat on the corner of the table near the door that he always entered. Then she heard his steps on the stairs way down on the first flight, and she turned white for just a moment. She had a habit of saying little silent prayers aloud about the simplest everyday things. Now she whispered: "Please, God, make him think that I am still pretty."

Jim stopped inside the door, as still as a setter at the scent of quail. His eyes were fixed upon Della. There was an expression on them that she could not read, and it terrified her. It was not anger, nor surprise, nor disapproval, nor horror, nor any of the feelings that she had been prepared for. He simply stared at her with that peculiar expression on his face.

Della wriggled off the table and went for him.

"Jim, darling," she cried, "don't look at me that way. I had my hair cut off and sold it because I couldn't have lived through Christmas without giving you a present. It'll grow again—you won't mind, will you? I just had to do it. My hair grows awfully fast. Say 'Merry Christmas!' and let's be happy. You don't know what a nice—what a beautiful, nice gift I've got for you."

"You've cut off your hair?" asked Jim, as if he had not arrived at that obvious fact even after the hardest mental labor.

"Cut it off and sold it," said Della. "Don't you like me just as well, anyhow? I'm me without my hair, ain't I?"

Jim looked about the room curiously.

"You say your hair is gone?" he asked in an upset voice.

"You needn't look for it," said Della. "It's sold, I tell you—sold and gone too. It's Christmas Eve, boy. Be good to me, for it went for you. Maybe the hairs of my head are numbered," she went on with a sudden serious expression, "but nobody could ever count my love for you. Shall I put the chops on, Jim?"

Jim drew a package from his overcoat pocket and threw it upon the table.

"Don't make any mistake, Dell," he said, "about me. I don't think there's anything in the way of a haircut or a shave or a shampoo that could make me like my girl any less. But if you'll unwrap that package, you may see why you had me going awhile at first."

Della's fingers tore at the string and paper. And then a scream of joy—and then, alas! A quick feminine change to hysterical tears and wails, requiring the immediate employment of all the comforting powers of the lord of the flat.

For there lay The Combs—the set of combs, side and back, that Della had worshipped for long in a Broadway shop window. Beautiful combs, pure tortoise-shell, with jeweled rims—just the shade to wear in the beautiful vanished hair. They were expensive combs, she knew, and her heart had simply craved and yearned over them without the least hope of possession. And now, they were hers, but the hair for which they should have been an ornament was gone.

She hugged them to her bosom. After a while, she was able to look up with dim eyes and a smile and say: "My hair grows so fast, Jim!"

And then Della leaped up like a little cat and cried, "Oh, oh!"

Jim had not yet seen his beautiful present. She held it out to him eagerly upon her open palm. The dull, precious metal chain seemed to flash with a reflection of her bright spirit.

"Isn't it a dandy, Jim?" Della Asked. "I hunted all over town to find it. You'll have to look at the time a hundred times a day now. Give me your watch. I want to see how it looks on it."

Instead of obeying, Jim tumbled down on the couch and put his hands under the back of his head and smiled.

"Dell," said he, "let's put our Christmas presents away and keep 'em a while. They're too nice to use just at present. I sold the watch to get the money to buy your combs. And now, suppose you put the chops on."

The magi, as you know, were wise men—wonderfully wise men—who brought gifts to the Babe in the manger. They gave the first Christmas gifts. Being wise, their gifts were no doubt wise ones. I have lamely told you the sad story of two foolish children who most unwisely sacrificed for each other their greatest treasures. But in a last word to the wise of these days, let this be said: Of all who give and receive gifts, these two were of the wisest. Everywhere they are wisest. They show the true meaning of giving and of love. They are the magi.

## READING FOR UNDERSTANDING

**1.** Arrange the following incidents in the order in which they occurred:

    **(a)** Della bought Jim a fob chain for his watch.

    **(b)** Jim returned home.

    **(c)** Jim told Della to put the chops on for dinner.

    **(d)** Della counted the money that she had saved.

    **(e)** Della rushed out to sell her hair.

**2.** What two possessions did Jim and Della treasure most?

**3.** Why did Della think that the platinum fob chain was the perfect gift for Jim?

**4.** Why did Jim act so strangely when he came home and saw Della?

**5.** Why did Della burst into tears when she saw the combs?

**6.** How do you think "The Gift of the Magi" reflects the values of the early 1900s?

## RESPONDING TO THE STORY

The characters in this story sell the most important things that they own. What is your most precious possession? Can you imagine any circumstances in which you would willingly part with it? Explain in a paragraph.

## REVIEWING VOCABULARY

Match each word on the left with the correct definition on the right.

| | |
|---|---|
| **1.** prudence | **a.** chain for a pocket watch |
| **2.** cascade | **b.** prevailing |
| **3.** ransacking | **c.** longed for |
| **4.** predominating | **d.** small, steep waterfall |
| **5.** fob chain | **e.** sound judgment |
| **6.** craved | **f.** searching well |
| **7.** platinum | **g.** precious metal |

## THINKING CRITICALLY

**1.** In the last paragraph of the story, O. Henry calls Jim and Della "two foolish children who most unwisely sacrificed for each other their greatest treasures." Then he writes that Jim and Della were wise, just like the magi. Explain in your own words why the author has made these two different statements.

**2.** Do you think this particular Christmas will affect the future of the young couple for the better or for the worse? Explain.

**3.** Is the title "The Gift of the Magi" a good one for this story? Why or why not?

# THE MOUSE

## adapted from a story by Saki

*The Scottish writer H. H. Munro lived from 1870 to 1916. During World War I, he fought in France and died there. While in London in 1908, he wrote many funny stories. Using the pen name* Saki, *he proved to be a master of the tale with a surprise ending. Many of his stories have a nasty sense of humor.*

*When Saki wrote, British society was formal. It valued upper-class manners and tastes. Saki loved making fun of such manners and tastes. Perhaps this is why he kept his real name a secret.*

*This story places a very proper man in a very silly situation. Trying to keep up his standards of politeness, he becomes very embarrassed. But in the end, something unexpected happens.*

## VOCABULARY WORDS

**coarser** (KAWR-suhr) more crude or rough
❖ In his second act, he told *coarser* jokes.

**slumber** (SLUM-buhr) to sleep
❖ After the basketball game, she was more inclined to *slumber* than to go out and celebrate.

**scrutiny** (SKROO-tuh-nee) close examination
❖ His testimony did not stand up to *scrutiny*.

**goaded** (GOHD-uhd) urged on
❖ Their insults *goaded* him to make an angry reply.

**improvised** (IHM-pruh-vyzd) made on the spur of the moment
❖ Using sheets and poles, they *improvised* a shelter.

**predicament** (prih-DIHK-uh-muhnt) unpleasant or embarrassing situation
❖ A cat caught in a tree is a common *predicament*.

## KEY WORD

**Providence** (PRAHV-uh-duhns) guiding power of the universe
❖ She said that *Providence* had guided her through hard times.

**T**heodoric **Voler** had been brought up by a doting mother. From the time he was an infant until he was well into middle age, her chief goal had been to protect him from what she called the coarser things of life. Anything that might upset or hurt him was considered a coarser thing of life. After she died, Theodoric found himself alone in a world that was a good deal more difficult to cope with than he thought it should be.

To Theodoric, even a simple train ride was full of annoyances and problems. As he settled himself down in a second-class compartment one September morning, he felt agitated and nervous.

He had been staying at the country residence of a minister and his family. These people were certainly pleasant enough, but they simply were not able to run an orderly household. Their inability to do so led only to trouble.

The day arrived when Theodoric had to return to London. But no one had sent for the pony cart that was to take him to the train station. When Theodoric was about to leave, the man who should have brought the cart was nowhere to be found.

In this emergency, Theodoric, to his dismay, had to join the minister's daughter in harnessing the pony. This stressful activity required moving about in a dark, damp stable. The stable smelled like an outhouse, except in those places where it smelled of mice.

Theodoric was not afraid of mice. Yet, he still thought of them as being among the coarser things of life. As such, they were to be avoided at all cost. Indeed, he felt that Providence might long ago have seen that mice were not needed and might have taken them away.

**51**

As the train left the station, Theodoric imagined that he gave off odors of a stable yard. He also feared that there might be a stale straw or two on his well-brushed clothes. Fortunately, the only other person in the compartment was a lady of about the same age as he. She seemed interested in slumber rather than scrutiny.

The train was not due to stop until the end of the line, in about an hour. And the old-fashioned carriage did not connect to a corridor. Therefore, no other travelers were likely to intrude on Theodoric's semiprivacy.

The train had barely reached its normal speed before he became aware that he was not alone with the sleeping lady. He was not even alone in his own clothes. A creeping movement over his skin told him of the presence of a mouse. It had evidently run into his clothes during the harnessing of the pony.

Stamps and shakes and pinches failed to remove the mouse. Theodoric lay back against the cushions. He was worn out by his efforts. His cheeks burned from the horror of it all. With all his might, he tried to think of some means to end the situation.

It was impossible for him to continue like this for a whole hour. On the other hand, nothing less than getting undressed would get rid of the mouse. To undress in the presence of a lady was an idea that filled him with deep shame.

And yet, the lady in this case seemed to be soundly asleep. The mouse, on the other hand, seemed to be trying to crowd a year's worth of exercise into a few minutes. Sometimes it lost its footing and slipped for half an inch or so. Then, in fright, or more probably temper, it bit. They were tiny bites. Yet each one sent a sharp pain through his body.

Theodoric was goaded into a bold move. In fact, it was the boldest move of his life. Once again his face reddened to the color of a beet. He kept an agonized watch on the sleeping woman. Then, quickly and quietly, he tied the ends of his railway blanket to the racks on either side.

A thick curtain now hung across the compartment. Thus, he had improvised a narrow dressing room. In this dressing room, he proceeded with great haste, urged on by those bites, to get himself partially and the mouse entirely out of his clothes.

As the mouse gave a wild leap to the floor, the blanket slipped and came down with a flop. Almost at the same time, the sleeping woman opened her eyes. With a movement quicker than the mouse's, Theodoric hauled the blanket chin-high over his half-dressed body as he fell into his seat.

Fear caused drops of sweat to form on his cheeks. The blood raced in the veins of his neck and forehead. His heart beat wildly, and he waited dumbly for the emergency cord to be pulled.

The lady, however, simply stared silently at her strangely dressed companion. Theodoric asked himself: "How much had she seen?" What on earth must she think of him in his present condition? The shame of it all was too much to bear. Desperate, he had to say something.

"I think I have caught a chill," he groaned.

"Really, I'm so sorry," she replied. "I was just going to ask if you would open this window."

"I think it must be malaria," he added. His teeth chattered from fright and from a strong desire to seem to be telling the truth.

"I've got some brandy in my bag, if you'll kindly hand it down to me," said his companion.

"Not for worlds—I mean, I never take anything for it," he assured her.

"I suppose you caught it in the tropics?"

Theodoric's knowledge of the tropics was limited to an annual present of tea from an uncle in Ceylon. Would it be possible, he wondered, to simply tell her the truth in small parts?

"Are you afraid of mice?" he asked, growing, if possible, more red in the face.

"Not unless they come in quantities." She looked puzzled. "Why do you ask?"

"I had one crawling inside my clothes just now," said Theodoric in a voice that hardly seemed his own. "It was a most awkward situation."

"It must have been, if you wear your clothes at all tight," she observed. "But mice have strange ideas of comfort."

"I had to get rid of it while you were asleep," he continued. Then, with a gulp, he added, "It was getting rid of it that brought me to—to this."

"Surely removing one small mouse wouldn't bring on a chill," she continued cheerily.

She must have guessed his predicament and was enjoying his confusion. An agony of embarrassment, worse than an army of mice, crept up and down over his soul.

Then, sheer terror took the place of shame. With every minute that passed, the train was rushing nearer to the crowded station. Dozens of prying eyes would replace her gaze.

There was one last chance. His fellow-traveler might go back to sleep. But as the minutes ticked by, that chance slipped away. The secret look that Theodoric stole at her from time to time revealed only that she was awake.

"I think we must be getting near our destination now," she remarked.

Theodoric had noted with growing alarm the groups of houses that meant they were coming to the end. The words acted as a signal.

Like a hunted beast breaking cover and dashing toward safety, he dropped the blanket and struggled into his clothes. He felt a choking sensation in his throat and heart. Sweat began to run down his face. There was an icy silence in that corner, toward which he dared not look.

Then, as he sank back in his seat, clothed and almost out of his mind, the train slowed down. The woman spoke.

"Would you be so kind," she asked, "as to get me a porter to put me into a cab? It's a shame to trouble you when you're feeling ill, but being blind makes one so helpless at a railway station."

## READING FOR UNDERSTANDING

1. Most of the story took place on a **(a)** ship **(b)** train **(c)** plane.
2. Theodoric was afraid that the lady on the train might **(a)** scream when she saw the mouse **(b)** leave him alone with the mouse **(c)** see him undress.
3. At first, he told the lady that he had a chill because he **(a)** often lied **(b)** was ashamed **(c)** was cold.
4. Then he told the truth because **(a)** the lady wanted to know it **(b)** his mother made him **(c)** he did not know enough about malaria to keep his lie going.
5. The lady never saw what happened because she was **(a)** blind **(b)** sad **(c)** old.

## RESPONDING TO THE STORY

Do you know anyone like Theodoric? Do you know people who worry too much about what others think? What does this story say about people who take themselves too seriously? Explain in a paragraph what you think of such people.

## REVIEWING VOCABULARY

The following sentences are based on the story. Decide which of the words following the sentences best fits each blank. Write your answers on a separate sheet of paper.

1. Theodoric had been protected from the _____ things in life.
2. He feared that _____ would reveal that he had no clothes on under the blanket.
3. When Theodoric thought about how to escape from his _____, he became embarrassed.

**4.** When the mouse bit him, he was _____ into action.

**5.** Using a blanket, he _____ a dressing room.

**6.** When the blanket fell, his companion awoke from her _____.

**Words:** *improvised, predicament, slumber, goaded, scrutiny, coarser*

## THINKING CRITICALLY

**1.** How would you describe the author's attitude toward Theodoric? Give evidence from the story to support your response. How does the author's attitude compare to your own?

**2.** Why did Theodoric tell the lady a lie about catching malaria? Why was this easier at first for him to say than telling her the truth?

**3.** How do you think the lady would have reacted if she were not blind?

# JADE SOUP: A FOLK TALE FROM CHINA

## adapted from a story by Carol Kendall and Yao-wen Li

*The story you are about to read is a folk tale from China. Folk tales are stories that people pass along from one generation to the next. The characters are usually ordinary people. See if you can recognize things about yourself or anyone else you know in the characters in the following story.*

*Folk tales entertain as well as teach. These tales usually combine a simple story with a comment on human nature. In this story, a very powerful man is about to learn an important lesson from a poor, wise old woman.*

*Read on to find out what lesson the man learns many years after he becomes Emperor of all China. What does the lesson teach you about the things that people desire?*

# VOCABULARY WORDS

**fortnight** (FAWRT-nyt) a period of two weeks
❖ She had waited for the package for a *fortnight*.

**dejection** (dih-JEHK-shuhn) depression; sadness
❖ By her look of *dejection*, I could tell that she had failed.

**ravenous** (RAV-uh-nuhs) very hungry
❖ The *ravenous* animal gobbled up the food.

**concocted** (kuhn-KAHKT-uhd) made by combining various ingredients creatively
❖ I couldn't figure out how they *concocted* that stew.

**ravishing** (RAV-ihsh-ihng) entrancing; delightful
❖ She recalled the *ravishing* view from the mountain.

**savory** (SAY-vuhr-ee) pleasing to the taste
❖ We enjoyed many *savory* dishes at his dinner party.

**zest** (ZEHST) exciting or stimulating quality
❖ The garlic adds *zest* to this chicken dish.

**rancid** (RAN-sihd) spoiled
❖ The smell of *rancid* butter made her feel sick.

# KEY WORDS

**dynasties** (DY-nuhs-teez) ruling families who pass on their power through the generations
❖ We studied the various *dynasties* that had ruled in China.

**bean curd** (BEEN KERD) a bland, cheese-like food made from soybeans, which are a rich source of protein
❖ At the Chinese restaurant, we ate fried *bean curd*.

**A** **thousand years ago and more,**
when China was split into "Five Dynasties
and Ten Kingdoms," the rulers could
scarcely get through a fortnight of peace
before a new war broke out and they lost
their thrones, or their heads, or both. Armies fought
back and forth across Central China in a bloody game
of Chinese chess. At last one great general outfought all
the others and himself became Emperor. But before the
final victory that changed General Zhao into Emperor
Zhao of the Song Dynasty, there were battles and
defeats enough to satisfy the most bloodthirsty. Of
course, there were not a few tales to tell along the way:
tales of courage, dejection, despair—and at least one of
near starvation.

It was during one of the early defeats, with his army
in confusion, that General Zhao became separated
from his men. The enemy was all about him. It was
unsafe to knock at any door. For three days Zhao hid in
ditches or hollows or behind rocks. He fled during the
dark hours from the region that meant certain death
should he be found there.

At last he reached the safe pine forests of a mountain. He breathed deeply the spicy air that meant freedom to the hunted. But pine needles could not feed a
starving man, and Zhao had not eaten since the defeat
of his army. Unless he found food soon, he would die
as surely as though the enemy had chopped him down.

Stumbling along a faint mountain path, scratched
and torn by thorns and nettles, he could think only of
food. So intense was his longing that he could actually
imagine the fragrance of cooking in the air he breathed.
The farther he staggered along the path, the stronger
came the scent, beckoning, luring him onward.

By the time he reached the other side of the forest, he was ravenous—and there by a crude hut, bending over a fire, was an old woman stirring the pot from which the delicious aroma rushed at him.

"Good grandmother . . . ," Zhao croaked.

The old woman turned and looked at him, at his torn clothes, his unshaven face, his trembling hands. Without a word, she dished up a bowl full of the bubbling stew—white bits of bean curd peeping through a bed of green vegetables. When he had gulped that down, she silently refilled the bowl and handed it to him.

Never had food tasted so good! "What . . . ," he mumbled through a mouthful of the savory morsels, ". . . what do you call this dish?"

"Oh, I call it Pearls Fallen on the Green Jade Tree," said the old woman. "But that is just my fancy. It is only a few bean curd bits and wild vegetables from the mountain. I live in a poor way."

"I shall never forget it," Zhao promised, "for it is the most wonderful meal of my life."

Many years passed. Zhao had long since swept away his enemies and proclaimed himself Emperor Taizu of the Middle Kingdom of China. Settled in his rich capital, he never wanted for food again. Delicacies were brought to his table from the mountains and the seas. Famous dishes from all over the kingdom were concocted for him. There was no gourmet delight he hadn't tasted.

Then, suddenly one day, he lost his appetite. He had had enough of exquisite dishes. No matter where they came from, they all ended up tasting the same. His mind wandered over his younger days, when all food tasted good because there was so little of it. Suddenly he remembered the old woman on the pine-clad mountain and the bowl of food she had given him—Pearls Fallen on the Green Jade Tree. Closing his eyes he could even now remember its ravishing taste. . . . If he could only recapture the ecstasy of that long-ago meal!

And why not? What were the royal cooks for if not to cater to his appetite? With rising excitement, he sent for all forty-seven of them. After describing the mountain woman's Pearls Fallen on the Green Jade Tree, he sent them all back to the kitchens, promising them rich rewards if they could produce the same dish.

The cooks set to with a will to please their Emperor's taste. They used only the choicest soybeans, grinding them exceedingly fine to make the soy milk, and setting the bean curd with great care. They went themselves to the kitchen gardens to pluck the freshest, greenest, most perfect vegetables. These they cooked with an excellent meat broth while the bean curd simmered in savory oil. When the dish was complete, they bore it to the Emperor's table in anticipation of the promised rich rewards.

The Emperor took one bite and threw down his chopsticks. "Tasteless! Boring! Dreary! How dare you call yourselves royal cooks. Even an old woman of the mountains puts your feeble dishes to shame! Get out, all of you!"

The next lot of cooks in the royal kitchen fared no better. They were dismissed so fast that their aprons were still clean when they left. There followed a procession of cooks through the palace kitchens—in one day, out the next—until the supply was exhausted. There was simply not a cook in the kingdom who could equal the old mountain woman's Pearls Fallen on the Green Jade Tree. The Emperor grew moody and sad. If he could only recapture the zest of those earlier days . . .

Meantime, the chief minister, seeing the chaos in the palace kitchens, had sent out runners to find the old woman of the mountains. At last they discovered her by her hut. She was still stirring her pot as though she hadn't moved from the spot all the years since the Emperor's visit when he was merely Zhao Kuangyin.

Bowing to the will of the Emperor now, but grumbling not a little at having her peace disturbed, she gathered together the ingredients for her jade soup and allowed herself and her big iron pot—the chief minister was not one to take chances with his Emperor's demands—to be transported to the capital city. There she was ushered into the palace kitchens, where she set up her pot. In went bits of dried bean curd, and when they had doubled in size, she poured in some rancid oil and stirred vigorously. Then she added water and threw in the wild grasses and leaves to cook.

In no time at all, the dish was ready for the Emperor Taizu. Emperor Taizu was more than ready to eat it. He loaded his chopsticks with a great helping and put it into his mouth.

Suddenly his eyes bulged and he gulped. Bitter, bitter! Water squeezed from between his eyelids and slid down his face. His tongue curled in his mouth. His teeth were full of grit. The portion that had plummeted into his stomach threatened to come up again.

"No, no!" he cried when he was able to talk. "It was not like that, not at all! You have forgotten how to cook that priceless dish!"

"Your Highness," said the woman with some impatience, "I have been cooking and eating that dish all my life, for I could never afford better. No, I have not forgotten. It is you who have forgotten how hungry you were on the day you came to my fire."

The Emperor stared at her as a sea of memories washed over him. "You are right," he said slowly. "I have forgotten. All of us here have forgotten. Good grandmother, I entreat you to prepare another pot of this same dish, just as you have always done. Tonight the whole court will dine on Pearls Fallen on the Green Jade Tree."

## READING FOR UNDERSTANDING

1. Arrange the following incidents in the order in which they occurred:
   (a) The Emperor ordered his cooks to make Pearls Fallen on the Green Jade Tree.
   (b) The Emperor lost his appetite.
   (c) The chief minister sent for the old woman.
   (d) General Zhao told the old woman that her soup was the most wonderful meal he had ever tasted.
   (e) General Zhao wandered through the forest.
2. Why do you think the old woman was silent when she gave Zhao the soup?
3. How did Zhao's life change when he became Emperor?
4. Why do you think the Emperor lost his appetite?
5. Why did the chief minister not want to take chances with the Emperor's demands?
6. How did the old woman feel about having to go to the capital city?

## RESPONDING TO THE STORY

Think back to a special meal or event in your life. What made it memorable? Write about your special event in a paragraph. Use descriptive language to re-create the experience.

## REVIEWING VOCABULARY

1. If you *concocted* a meal, you (a) combined various ingredients in a new way (b) ordered it from a restaurant (c) ate it quickly.
2. A person with a look of *dejection* probably (a) won a contest (b) lost a dear friend (c) feels hungry.

**3.** If a meal is *ravishing*, it is **(a)** spicy **(b)** delightful **(c)** raw.

**4.** A spice that adds *zest* is **(a)** dull **(b)** exciting **(c)** expensive.

**5.** A *fortnight* is two **(a)** days **(b)** weeks **(c)** months.

**6.** If food is *rancid*, you would **(a)** buy more **(b)** throw it out **(c)** serve it at a party.

**7.** Someone who is *ravenous* **(a)** will eat a lot **(b)** will eat a little **(c)** is not hungry.

**8.** If you taste something *savory*, you would probably **(a)** not finish it **(b)** ask for more **(c)** store it in the freezer.

## THINKING CRITICALLY

**1.** Compare the Emperor's second reaction to the old woman's soup with the first time he tasted it. What had changed in Zhao's life? Why was his reaction different the second time? What lesson had he learned?

**2.** How would you describe Zhao's character? List three of his character traits. Then tell which of his actions revealed each of these traits.

# THE NECKLACE

## adapted from a story by Guy de Maupassant

*Guy de Maupassant was a sharp observer of French life during the late nineteenth century. He had the ability to enter his characters' minds and make the reader aware of their most burning desires. In the following story, the woman, more than anything, wants to be something she is not. She wants to be richer, better dressed, and more stylish than she can afford.*

*For one evening only, her fairy tale dream comes true. She gets the chance to experience the pleasures of a "fashionable lady." Unfortunately, she must pay a high price for this one evening. Something unexpected happens that changes her life forever. It will be up to you to decide if this change is for the better or the worse.*

## VOCABULARY WORDS

**dowry** (DOW-ree) money property brought to a marriage by the bride
❖ Because the woman's family was poor, she had no *dowry*.

**vexed** (VEHKST) annoyed
❖ His constant complaining *vexed* us.

**vestibule** (VEHS-tuh-byool) small entrance hall
❖ Just inside the main entrance door was a small *vestibule*, where visitors took off their overcoats.

**bewilderment** (bih-WIHL-duhr-muhnt) confusion
❖ His puzzled frown clearly showed his *bewilderment*.

## KEY WORDS

**M. and Mme.** abbreviations for Monsieur (muh-SYER) and Madame (muh-DAHM)
❖ She accepted the invitation of *M.* and *Mme.* Caron.

**francs** (FRANGKS) basic units of French money
❖ The pastry cost three *francs*.

**Seine** (SAYN) a river that runs through Paris
❖ The couple finally found a taxicab by the *Seine*.

**Palais-Royal** (pa-LAY roi-YAL) a famous group of buildings in Paris
❖ When we were in Paris, we visited the *Palais-Royal*.

**sous** (SOO) old French coins
❖ Twenty *sous* used to equal one franc.

**Champs Elysées** (shahn zay-lee-ZAY) the most famous avenue in Paris
❖ Every year on July 14, the French national holiday, there is a large parade down the *Champs Elysées*.

**S**he was one of those pretty, charming young ladies, born, as if through an error of fate, into a family of clerks. She had no dowry and no hopes, and she allowed herself to marry an unimportant clerk in the office of the Board of Education.

She suffered constantly, thinking that she should be leading a stylish life of luxury. She suffered from the poverty of her apartment, the shabby walls, and the worn chairs. All of these things, which another woman in her position would not have noticed, tortured and angered her.

One evening, her husband returned, overjoyed, bearing in his hand a large envelope.

"Here," he said, "here is something for you."

She quickly tore open the envelope and pulled out a printed card, on which the following words were written:

> *The Minister of Public Instruction and*
> *Madame George Ramponneau ask the*
> *honor of M. and Mme. Loisel's company*
> *Monday evening, January 18, at the*
> *Minister's residence.*

Instead of being delighted, as her husband had hoped, she frowned and threw the invitation on the table, murmuring, "What do you suppose I would want with that?"

"But, my dearie, I thought it would make you happy. You never go out, and this is an occasion, and a fine one! I had a great deal of trouble getting this invitation. Everybody wants one, but few can get them. Not many are given to employees. You will see the whole official world there."

She looked at him with an irritated eye and declared impatiently, "What do you suppose I have to wear to such a thing as that?"

He had not thought of that. He stammered, "Why, the dress you wear when we go to the theater. It seems very pretty to me."

He was dismayed at the sight of his wife weeping. Two great tears fell slowly from the corners of her eyes. He stammered, "What is the matter? What is the matter?"

By much effort, she controlled her irritation and responded in a calm voice, wiping her moist cheeks: "Nothing. Only I have no dress, and consequently I cannot go to this affair. Give your card to some colleague whose wife is better dressed than I."

He was grieved but answered, "Let us see, Matilda. How much would a suitable dress cost, something that would serve for other occasions, something very simple?"

She reflected for some seconds. Finally she said in a hesitating voice, "I cannot tell exactly, but it seems to me that four hundred francs ought to cover it."

"Very well, I will give you four hundred francs. But try to find a pretty dress."

As the day of the ball approached, Mme. Loisel seemed sad, disturbed, anxious. Nevertheless, her dress was nearly ready. Her husband said to her one evening, "What is the matter with you? You have acted strangely for two or three days."

And she answered, "I am vexed not to have a jewel, not one stone, nothing to set off my beauty. I shall have such a poverty-stricken look. I would prefer not to go to this party."

Then her husband suggested, "Go and find your friend Madame Forestier, and ask her to lend you some of her jewels! You are well enough acquainted with her to do this."

She uttered a cry of joy. "It is true!" she said. "I had not thought of that."

The next day, she took herself to her friend's house and related her story of distress. Madame Forestier went to her closet with the glass doors, took out a large jewel case, brought it, opened it, and said: "Choose, my dear."

She saw at first some bracelets, then a necklace of pearls, then a Venetian cross of gold and jewels. She tried all the jewels before the mirror, hesitated, and could neither decide to take them nor leave them. Then she asked, "Have you nothing more?"

"Why, yes. Look for yourself. I do not know what will please you."

She discovered in a black satin box a superb necklace of diamonds, and her heart beat fast with desire. Her hands trembled as she took them up. She placed them about her throat, against her dress, and remained in ecstasy before them. Then she asked in a hesitating voice full of anxiety:

"Could you lend me this? Only this?"

"Why, yes, certainly."

She fell upon the neck of her friend, embraced her with passion, then went away with her treasure.

The day of the ball arrived. Mme. Loisel was a great success. She was the prettiest of all—elegant, gracious, smiling and full of joy. All the members of the Cabinet wished to waltz with her. Even the minister of education paid attention to her.

She danced with enthusiasm, with passion, intoxicated with pleasure, thinking of nothing. She danced in a kind of cloud of happiness that came of all this honor and all this admiration.

She went home at nearly four o'clock in the morning. Her husband put around her shoulders the wraps that they had carried for the journey home. They were modest garments for everyday wear. They clashed with the elegant ball costume. When they were in the street, they found no carriage. They began to look for one, hailing the coachmen whom they saw at a distance. They walked along the Seine, hopeless and shivering. Finally they found an old cab that took them as far as their door on Martyr Street, and they went wearily up to their apartment.

She removed the wraps from her shoulders before the mirror for a final view of herself in her glory. Suddenly she uttered a cry! Her necklace was not around her neck!

Her husband, already half undressed, asked, "What is the matter?"

She turned toward him excitedly. "I have—I have—I no longer have Madame Forestier's necklace!"

He arose in dismay. "What! How is that? It is not possible."

And they looked in the folds of the dress, in the pockets, everywhere. They could not find it.

He asked, "You are sure you still had it when we left the house?"

"Yes, I felt it as we came out through the vestibule."

"But if you had lost it in the street, we would have heard it fall. It must be in the cab."

"Yes, that is probable. Did you take the number?"

"No. And you, did you notice what it was?"

"No."

They looked at each other, horribly upset. Finally, Loisel dressed himself again.

"I am going," said he, "back to the area where we went on foot, to see if I can find it."

And he went. She remained in her evening gown, not having the strength to go to bed, stretched upon a chair, without ambition or thoughts.

Toward seven o'clock, her husband returned. He had found nothing.

He went to the police and to the cab offices and put an advertisement in the newspapers, offering a reward if the necklace was returned. He did everything that could offer them a shred of hope.

She waited all day in a state of fright and bewilderment. Loisel returned in the evening, with his face anxious and pale, having discovered nothing.

"It will be necessary," said he, "to write to your friend and tell her that you have broken the clasp of the necklace and that you will have it repaired. That will give us time."

She wrote as he dictated.

At the end of a week, they had lost all hope. And Loisel, older by five years, declared, "We must take measures to replace the necklace."

They went from jeweler to jeweler, seeking a necklace like the other one, consulting their memories—ill, both of them, with anxiety.

In a shop at the Palais-Royal, they found a necklace of diamonds which seemed to them exactly like the one they had lost. It was valued at forty thousand francs. They could get it for thirty-six thousand.

They begged the jeweler not to sell it for three days. And they made an arrangement by which they might return it for thirty-four thousand francs if they found the other one before the end of February.

Loisel possessed eighteen thousand francs which his father had left him. He borrowed the rest.

When Mme. Loisel took back the jewels to Mme. Forestier, the latter said to her coldly, "You should have returned them to me sooner. I might have needed them."

She did not open the jewel box as her friend feared she would. If she should notice the substitution, what would she think? What should she say? Would she take her for a robber?

Mme. Loisel now knew the horrible life of necessity. She did her part, however, with courage. It was necessary to pay this frightful debt. She would pay it. They discharged the maid, and they changed their apartment.

She learned all the tiresome tasks of being a maid, and doing housework. She worked hard in the kitchen. She washed the dishes, using her rosy nails upon the greasy pots and the bottoms of the stewpans.

The husband worked evenings, putting the books of some merchants in order, and at night he often did copying at five sous a page.

And this life lasted for ten years.

At the end of ten years, they had restored all, all, including the moneylender's interest, and compound interest besides. Mme. Loisel seemed old now. She had become a strong, hard woman.

But sometimes, when her husband was at the office, she would seat herself before the window and think of that evening party of long ago, of that ball where she was so beautiful and so flattered.

How would it have been if she had not lost that necklace? Who knows? Who knows? How odd life is and how full of changes! How small a thing will ruin or save one!

One Sunday, as she was taking a walk in the Champs Elysees to rid herself of the cares of the week, she suddenly noticed a woman walking with a child. It was Mme. Forestier, still young, pretty, and attractive.

She approached her. "Good morning, Jeanne."

Her friend did not recognize her and was astonished to be so familiarly addressed by this common person. She stammered, "But, madame, I do not know you. You must be mistaken."

"No, I am Matilda Loisel."

Her friend uttered a cry of astonishment. "Oh! my poor Matilda! How you have changed."

"Yes, I have had some hard days since I saw you, and some miserable ones—and all because of you."

"Because of me? How is that?"

"You recall the diamond necklace that you loaned me to wear to the minister's ball?"

"Yes, very well."

"Well, I lost it."

"How is that, since you returned it to me?"

"I returned another exactly like it to you. And it has taken us ten years to pay for it. You can understand that it was not easy for us, who have nothing. But it is finished, and I am decently content."

Mme. Forestier stopped short. She said, "You say that you bought a diamond necklace to replace mine?"

"Yes. You did not notice it then? They were just alike."

And she smiled with a proud and simple joy. Mme. Forestier was touched and took both of her hands as she replied, "Oh, my poor Matilda! Mine were false. They were not worth over five hundred francs!"

# READING FOR UNDERSTANDING

The following paragraphs summarize the story. Decide which of the words below the paragraphs best fits in each blank. Write your answers on a separate sheet of paper.

Mme. Loisel was married to a **(1)**_____ and lived in an **(2)**_____. One evening, her husband returned home with an **(3)**_____ to a **(4)**_____. She bought a new **(5)**_____ to wear and borrowed a diamond **(6)**_____ from a friend. At the party, she was a big **(7)**_____.

When the couple reached home, however, they discovered that the necklace was **(8)**_____. All their **(9)**_____ to find it failed. They paid a **(10)**_____ thirty-six thousand **(11)**_____ for a **(12)**_____. M. Loisel took out many **(13)**_____. Both he and his wife worked for ten **(14)**_____ to earn the **(15)**_____ to pay off the loans.

Finally, when the whole **(16)**_____ had been paid, Mme. Loisel met her **(17)**_____ out on a **(18)**_____. When she confessed the **(19)**_____ about the necklace, her friend replied that the lost diamonds were **(20)**_____.

**Words:** *efforts, party, loans, debt, clerk, necklace, invitation, walk, money, fake, dress, apartment, missing, success, friend, replacement, jeweler, years, truth, francs*

# RESPONDING TO THE STORY

Choose one scene, event, or statement in this story that made a strong impression on you. What made the situation or statement meaningful to you? Explain in a paragraph.

## REVIEWING VOCABULARY

**1.** A *vexed* person is **(a)** annoyed **(b)** unlucky **(c)** wealthy.

**2.** His look of *bewilderment* showed that he **(a)** understood the game **(b)** didn't understand the game **(c)** was angry at the players.

**3.** The woman's lack of a *dowry* pointed to her family's **(a)** poverty **(b)** high social position **(c)** foreign status.

**4.** The *vestibule* of the minister's house was a **(a)** tiny corridor in the basement **(b)** flight of steps leading to the attic **(c)** small entrance hall.

## THINKING CRITICALLY

**1.** What is there about Matilda's behavior at the beginning of the story that might make her seem like a superficial person? Does she change over the course of the story? If so, how?

**2.** What is your idea of Mme. Forestier's real character? What details do you find out about her that influence your opinion?

**3.** Near the end of the story, Matilda Loisel thinks how strange life is. Do you agree with her that a small thing can ruin or save a person? Use examples from your reading or from real life to support your opinion.

# Unit 3
## THE UNEXPECTED

# LOVE AND LASAGNA

## Jeffrey Cooper

*How would you define love or the process of falling in love? What makes one person feel attracted to another?*

*If you're like most people, you'll probably agree that love is an age-old mystery. Where does the feeling come from? What does it mean? Love is wonderful, but it's also puzzling and maybe a little scary at the same time. It has been known to cause people to behave in strange ways.*

*In the following story, Jasmine is eager to find love. But though she may yearn for it, she can't just make love happen. Love is one of life's miracles, like the changing seasons. You can't hurry them along or make them last longer than they do. One thing is certain: When you try to force love, you may get unexpected results.*

# VOCABULARY WORDS

**lasagna** (luh-ZAHN-yuh) pasta with layers of tomato sauce, ground meat, and cheese
❖ We enjoyed a truly delicious *lasagna* dinner at Juan's beach house.

**quarterback** (KWAWR-tuhr-bak) player who calls the signals and offensive plays in football
❖ Craig was the star *quarterback* of his football team.

**impish** (IHM-pihsh) mischievous, playful
❖ With an *impish* grin, Trudi said that she had played a joke on us.

**aroma** (uh-ROH-muh) smell
❖ The *aroma* of freshly baked bread spread throughout the large house.

**concealed** (kuhn-SEELD) hidden
❖ The card was *concealed* in her boot, so she never was able to find it.

# KEY WORD

**Kwanzaa** (KWAHN-zuh) African American holiday that begins on December 26 and continues through January 1.
❖ The holiday of *Kwanzaa* celebrates the accomplishments and achievements of African Americans.

**J**asmine had been looking forward to Khadijah's party all week. It was to be a Kwanzaa party.

After six months at Oakdale High, she still thought of herself as the new kid in town. The only friend that she had made so far was a girl named Shanene who sat at her lab table in biology class. Khadijah sat at their table, too. He was very nice, but he wasn't her type. However, Jasmine was delighted that she and Shanene had been invited to his house for a traditional Kwanzaa celebration. It would be a great way to make new friends. She decided to bring a sweet potato pie to help celebrate the harvest festival.

At the party, she recognized many people from school, including the star quarterback of the football team and the girl who had led the debating team to victory. Jasmine smiled at the handsome quarterback when he looked her way, and she felt her heart flutter when the boy smiled back. Now *there's* someone I wouldn't mind getting to know a whole lot better, she thought with an impish grin.

It was the inviting aroma of freshly baked garlic bread that drew Jasmine toward the kitchen. Standing in the doorway, she could see Khadijah and his best friend, Tedrick, sitting at a small table. The boys sat with their backs to the doorway, and neither of them realized that Jasmine was standing there and listening in on their conversation.

"I still think it's a crazy idea," Tedrick said to Khadijah. "If you like the girl so much, why don't you just tell her to her face?"

"You know how it is," said Khadijah. "It's hard asking someone out for the first time, especially when you hardly even know the girl."

"You're right about that," said Tedrick, "but putting a note in the lasagna is just too weird! What are you going to do if she swallows it?"

"I'm not putting it in the *lasagna*," said Khadijah. He picked up a large dinner napkin and carefully folded it around a pale blue note card. "See, it'll be tucked inside her napkin. When she opens the napkin, she'll see the note."

Jasmine ducked back into the living room just as Tedrick began to turn around. She wondered which of the girls at the party was going to find a secret message from Khadijah hidden in her napkin. Would it be the beautiful captain of the debating team? Or the tall girl in the red dress? Jasmine had seen Khadijah talking to her at lunch the other day. Maybe it would be Shanene. That would be nice, she thought. She knew that Shanene was still feeling low about breaking up with her longtime boyfriend. Khadijah seemed like a terrific person, and Jasmine knew that Shanene liked him. Going out with Khadijah might be just the thing to lift her sagging spirits, Jasmine decided.

"Dinner's ready," announced Khadijah, interrupting Jasmine's thoughts. She followed the others into the kitchen. Khadijah and Tedrick were standing next to the table now. As the guests filed by, Tedrick handed each one a plate brimming with lasagna and garlic bread. Khadijah then gave each person a knife and fork neatly wrapped inside a dinner napkin.

Jasmine fell into line behind Shanene. She watched closely as Khadijah handed Shanene her folded napkin. Was hers the napkin with the note hidden inside? Jasmine couldn't tell.

Jasmine took her own napkin and silverware, and followed Shanene back into the living room. Most of the others had already seated themselves on the floor around the large coffee table in the center of the room. Jasmine joined Shanene on the small sofa in the far corner of the room. Jasmine watched closely as her friend shook open her napkin and arranged it on her lap. There was nothing inside the napkin except a knife and a fork.

Jasmine looked around the room. Everyone was busy eating. No one was studying a pale blue note card with a secret message from Khadijah written inside.

He must have changed his mind at the last minute, Jasmine thought, as she reached for her silverware. It was then that she noticed the pale blue note card concealed within her neatly folded napkin.

*Me?* she thought. *There must be some kind of mistake!* She looked up and saw Khadijah sitting next to Tedrick at the other end of the room. He was looking right at her, and there was a big smile on his face.

Jasmine quickly looked away. She liked Khadijah a lot, but she had never imagined him as a possible boyfriend. True, he was good-looking, intelligent, and had a wonderful sense of humor, and it had been a long time since she had gone out on a date with someone she really liked. She was more interested in the football player, however. If only it were he who had sent her the note! Still, who knew what might happen before the evening was over? Jasmine imagined herself chatting with the handsome quarterback, smiling sweetly as he asked her if she had any plans for Saturday night. If only Khadijah had sent his note to Shanene, she thought, everything would have been so much simpler.

Then Jasmine decided to take matters into her own hands. When Shanene wasn't looking, Jasmine slipped the pale blue note card out of her napkin and casually dropped it on the sofa.

"What's that?" Jasmine asked innocently.

"What's what?" asked Shanene.

"That card," said Jasmine. "I saw it fall out of your napkin."

"Really?" Shanene picked up the note card and looked inside. Jasmine tried not to grin as her friend's jaw dropped in amazement.

"What is it?" asked Jasmine. Shanene handed her the note.

> *Would you go out with me Saturday night?*
> *Khadijah*

Both girls looked across the room at Khadijah. He looked very uncomfortable and was whispering something to Tedrick. Tedrick just looked at the two girls and grinned.

"What should I do?" whispered Shanene.

"Go over there and talk to him," said Jasmine. "Tell him that you'd be happy to go out with him on Saturday night."

"But Khadijah and I are just friends!" Shanene insisted.

"That's perfect," said Jasmine. "What could be more natural than a couple of friends going out together on a Saturday night?"

"Are you sure this fell out of my napkin?" asked Shanene, re-reading the note.

"I saw it with my own two eyes," Jasmine lied. "What's the problem, anyway? I thought you said Khadijah was a wonderful guy."

"He is," said Shanene. "As a matter of fact, I always thought that he would be just perfect for *you*. You two would make a great couple."

"For *me*?" asked Jasmine. She was amazed by her friend's words.

"Sure. The two of you have so much in common. But, as long as he sent this sweet note to *me*, I suppose I'd be foolish not to accept. Thanks, Jasmine!"

Shanene put down her plate and crossed the room. Jasmine watched as Tedrick got up and Shanene sat down next to Khadijah. At first, Khadijah looked very unhappy as Shanene began talking to him with the note card clutched in her hand. Then he began to relax, and a warm smile spread across his face. Jasmine wondered why she had never before noticed how handsome Khadijah was. She watched as Shanene gently touched the boy's hand. Then they both laughed, and Shanene leaned forward to peck Khadijah on the cheek. By the time she came back to Jasmine, Shanene seemed to be glowing with happiness.

"Guess who has a date with a really special guy Saturday night?" she asked, her eyes sparkling.

Not me, thought Jasmine, trying hard to look pleased for her friend. She glanced at the football player and saw him sitting hand in hand with the captain of the debating team. Like everyone else in the room, they seemed to be extremely happy together.

In fact, everybody seemed to be having a good time except Jasmine. But she didn't want anyone to know the mistake she had just made. With a stiff smile, she lifted a forkful of Khadijah's lasagna to her lips and tasted it. Across the room, Khadijah had started to look even more handsome. And he was a pretty good cook, as well.

## READING FOR UNDERSTANDING

**1.** The story took place **(a)** on Thanksgiving **(b)** on New Year's Eve **(c)** at a Kwanzaa party.

**2.** Jasmine was eager to attract **(a)** Tedrick **(b)** Khadijah **(c)** the star quarterback.

**3.** Khadijah let Jasmine know how he felt about her by **(a)** telling Tedrick **(b)** inviting her to the party **(c)** sending her a note, asking her out.

**4.** Jasmine was surprised to find the card in her napkin because she **(a)** never thought of Khadijah as a boyfriend **(b)** does not want a boyfriend **(c)** knows that Khadijah likes Shanene.

**5.** Khadijah was unhappy when Shanene approached him with the note card because **(a)** she was Tedrick's girlfriend **(b)** he gave the card to Jasmine **(c)** he had to leave quickly.

**6.** At the end of the story, Jasmine realized that she **(a)** acted well **(b)** attracted the quarterback **(c)** lost out on a wonderful date.

## RESPONDING TO THE STORY

What do you think about Jasmine's actions in the story? Do you think she was right to deceive her friend Shanene in this way? Why or why not? Use evidence from the story to support your view.

## REVIEWING VOCABULARY

The following sentences are based on the story. Decide which of the words following the sentences best fits each blank. Write your answers on a separate sheet of paper.

**1.** Jasmine could smell the _____ of the sweet potato pie that she baked for the party.

**2.** She was pleased when the _____ smiled at her.

**3.** She saw how the boys _____ a note card in a napkin.

**4.** Jasmine had an _____ look on her face when she thought about the football player.

**5.** Khadijah served his guests large portions of _____.

**Words:**  *concealed, quarterback, aroma, lasagna, impish*

## THINKING CRITICALLY

**1.** Jasmine knows that Khadijah is good-looking and intelligent and has a great sense of humor. Yet she rejects the chance to go out with him. How do you explain her behavior?

**2.** After Jasmine plays a trick on Shanene and Khadijah, her feelings for Khadijah change. How does she feel about him at the end of the story? How does the author express these emotions?

**3.** Imagine how you would continue the story. Would Jasmine try to win Khadijah back? What kinds of actions would she take? How would she deal with Shanene?

# UNICORN
## by Peter Dickinson

*Irish folk tales and legends are full of many fantastic creatures such as dragons and mermaids. In this story, you will meet a unicorn in the Ireland of long ago. A unicorn looks much like a horse, but it has a horn in the center of its forehead. Many people used to believe that such a creature had strange and wonderful powers.*

*What would you do if you came face to face with a unicorn? Would you be scared or would you be excited? The little girl in this story develops a special friendship with a unicorn that she meets. Why the unicorn is attracted to her is something of a mystery.*

*The story ends with a dramatic, rather bloody scene. What will happen to the little girl and her magical friend from the forest? To find out, read on.*

## VOCABULARY WORDS

**farthing** (FAWR-thihng) an old British coin with little value

❖ The miser wouldn't even part with a *farthing*.

**foal** (FOHL) a young horse

❖ The *foal* stood close to its mother in the barn.

**cavorting** (kuh-VAWRT-ihng) romping around happily

❖ The children were *cavorting* with the puppies.

**entranced** (ehn-TRANST) charmed; filled with delight

❖ We were *entranced* by the pretty little girl's song.

**bellowing** (BEHL-oh-ihng) calling out loudly; roaring

❖ The bear was *bellowing* in rage as the hunters took her cub.

**maiden** (MAYD-uhn) an unmarried girl or young woman

❖ As the *maiden* sat in the garden, she heard the knight singing of his love for her.

**heir** (EHR) anyone who inherits property from a person who has died

❖ After the king died, his *heir* received the castle, the land, and all the jewels.

## KEY WORDS

**truffles** (TRUF-uhls) dark fungus that grows underground and is used as food

❖ At the restaurant, each dish had a *truffle* on top.

**basilisks** (BAS-uh-lihsks) mythical lizardlike monsters who can kill with their breath or a glance

❖ The old book had pictures of knights fighting the *basilisks*.

**R**hiannon was an orphan. She lived with her grandmother in a village at the edge of the forest. She was one of Sir Brangwyn's orphans, as they called them in those parts—that is to say, her parents were alive but her father was imprisoned in the dungeons of Castle Grim. Her mother worked in the castle kitchens to earn money to pay for his food. He had done nothing wrong. But Sir Brangwyn had accused him of stealing deer. Sir Brangwyn liked to have the best men from all the villages in his dungeons, so that the other villagers would stay quiet and good, and hardly dare murmur when he taxed them of every farthing they had. Everyone knew that Rhiannon's father was innocent. If he had really been stealing deer, Sir Brangwyn would have hanged him from the nearest tree.

Rhiannon was not allowed to go with her parents to the castle. Sir Brangwyn made a point of leaving the children behind, to remind the other villagers to be good. So she stayed in the village and did her share of the work. Everybody in the village had to work or starve. Since Rhiannon was only nine, her job was to hunt in the forest for truffles.

The forest was enormous—nobody knew how big, or what lay deep inside it. Some said that strange beasts laired there, dragons and unicorns and basilisks, which could turn you to stone by looking at you. Others said all that had happened in the old days, and the strange beasts were gone, so now there were only ordinary animals such as boars and deer and wolves and bears. Sometimes Sir Brangwyn would come and hunt these. Hunting was the one thing he cared about in all the world.

Rhiannon never went deep into the forest. She

always stayed where she could see the edge. Truffles are hard to find. They are a leathery black fungus which grows underground on the roots of certain trees. For those who like rich food (as Sir Brangwyn did), they add a particularly delicious taste and smell. Rhiannon always hoped that one day she would find so many truffles that Sir Brangwyn would send her parents home as a reward. But it did not happen. She seldom found more than a few. Sometimes she would dig in forty places and find none.

Exactly a year after the soldiers had come to take her father away, Rhiannon went off to the forest as usual. But not at all as usual, she was followed back that evening by a small white horse. It was no more than a foal, pure silvery white with a silky mane and tail.

The villagers were amazed.

"It must have escaped from some lord's stable," they said. They tried to catch it, thinking there would be a reward. But before they came anywhere near, away it darted, glimmering across the meadows and into the dark woods. Then they found, to their further amazement, that Rhiannon's basket was full of truffles.

"My little horse showed me where to dig," she said.

This seemed very good news. Sir Brangwyn's tax-clerk would be coming to the village in a few days' time. Truffles were rare and expensive. Perhaps they could pay all their taxes in truffles. That would mean they would have a little food to spare for themselves this year. So next morning a dozen men and women went up with Rhiannon to the forest. They hoped the little horse would come and show them where to dig. But they saw no sign of it and they found nothing for themselves. At noon they went back to their own tasks, leaving Rhiannon behind. Again that evening the white

horse came glimmering behind her almost to the edge of the village, then dashed away. And again Rhiannon's basket was full of truffles.

So it went on every day until the tax-clerk came, and the headman brought him a whole sackload of truffles to pay the taxes. This clerk was a monk, who could read and write. He knew things which ordinary people do not know. When he asked how it happened that the village had so many truffles to send, the headman told him. The headman was a simple fellow. (Sir Brangwyn saw to it that the clever ones were in his dungeons.)

That evening the clerk sent for a huntsman and told him what he wanted. The next night the huntsman came back and told what he had seen. He had followed Rhiannon up to the forest, taking care to keep out of sight. At the forest edge a little white horse had come cavorting out and kissed Rhiannon on the forehead. Then she had followed it in under the trees where it had run to and fro, sniffling and snuffling like a dog. Every now and then it would stop and paw with its hoof on the ground, and Rhiannon would dig there and find truffles. The horse was obviously extremely shy of anyone but Rhiannon and kept looking nervously around. The huntsman had not been able to come close. But then, when Rhiannon's basket was full, she had sat down with her back against a tree and the horse had knelt by her side and put its head in her lap and gazed into her eyes and she had sung to it. The little horse had been so entranced that it seemed to forget all danger, and the huntsman had been able to creep close enough to see it well.

"And sure, it's a very fine wee beast, your honor," he said to the clerk. "What it'll be doing in these woods I can't be guessing. And it's never seen bit nor bridle, I'll be bound, never seen stall nor stable. As for the color of its coat, it is whiter than snow, not a touch nor fleck of gray nor of yellow in it. Only one thing . . ."

"Yes?" whispered the clerk, as though he knew what was coming.

"The pity of it is the animal's face, for it's mis-shapen. It has this lump, or growth as it might be, big as my bent thumb between the eyes."

"Ah," said the clerk.

Next morning he left his tax-gathering and hurried to Castle Grim to tell Sir Brangwyn there was a unicorn in the woods.

The great hall of Castle Grim was hung with the trophies of Sir Brangwyn's hunting. Deer and hare, boar and badger, wolf and fox, heron and dove, he had ridden it down or dug it up or hawked it out of the air. But he had never hunted unicorn. Before the clerk had finished his message, Sir Brangwyn was on his feet and bellowing for his huntsmen and his grooms. In an hour he was on the road with a dozen expert trackers and twenty couple of hounds.

The people of Rhiannon's village were glad to see him come. Sometimes when a village had shown him good sport he had let the people off their taxes for a whole year. So here they were eager to help. They beat the woods, they dug traps where they were told, and they set watch. But it was all no use. Sir Brangwyn's clever hounds bayed to and fro and found nothing. His trackers found the prints of an unshod foal all over the truffle-grounds, but lost the trail among the trees.

After three days of this, Sir Brangwyn's temper soured. The villagers began to be anxious. Then the tax-clerk said what Sir Brangwyn had been too impatient to hear before. He explained that the only way to hunt a unicorn is to send a maiden alone into the woods. The unicorn will come to her and lay its head

**94**

in her lap and be so enraptured by her singing that he will not see the huntsmen coming.

Sir Brangwyn had not brought any maidens with him, but the village headman told him about Rhiannon. All that night the villagers toiled by torch-light, cutting brushwood and building a great bank of it by the truffle-grounds, high enough to  hide a mounted man. In the morning they took Rhiannon up to the forest. When they told her what she had to do, she tried to say no. But by this time Sir Brangwyn had learnt where her parents were, and he explained to her what would happen to them if she refused. So she went into the forest and sat down, weeping, in her usual place. Meanwhile, Sir Brangwyn waited behind the bank of brushwood.

For a long while everything was still.

Then, suddenly, there was a glimmering deep in the dark wood. The unicorn came delicately out, looking this way and that, hesitating, sniffing the wind. When it was sure all was safe it cavorted up to Rhiannon and kissed her on the forehead and knelt by her side with its head on her lap, gazing up into her eyes, puzzled why she did not sing. Sir Brangwyn broke from his hide, spurring the sides of his horse till the blood run-nelled. The nearing hooves drubbed like thunder.

Then Rhiannon could bear it no more. She jumped to her feet with her arms round the unicorn's neck, dragging it up, and turned its head so that it could see Sir Brangwyn coming.

At once it reared away, giving Rhiannon no time to loose her hold. The movement twitched her sideways and up so that she was lying along the unicorn's back with her arms round its neck. The unicorn was darting away under the trees with Sir Brangwyn hallooing behind, his spear poised for the kill.

**95**

The hoofbeats dwindled into the forest, into silence. Then huntsmen and villagers, waiting out of sight beyond the forest, heard a voice like the snarl of trumpets, a man's shout and a crash. Then silence once more.

The trackers followed the hoofprints deep into the dark wood. They found Sir Brangwyn's body under an oak tree, pierced through from side to side. His horse they caught wandering close by.

Rhiannon came out of the forest at sunset. What had she seen and heard? What fiery eye, what silvery mane? What challenge and what charge? She would not say.

Only when her mother and father came home, set free by Sir Brangwyn's heir, she told them something. They had taken her to her bed and were standing looking down at her, full of their happiness in being all three together again, and home, when she whispered four words.

"Unicorns have parents, too."

## READING FOR UNDERSTANDING

**1.** How old was Rhiannon, and what was her job?

**2.** Where were Rhiannon's parents, and what did they do?

**3.** Why did Sir Brangwyn want to put all the clever men in his dungeon?

**4.** What was the only thing Sir Brangwyn cared about?

**5.** Why does the author use *glimmering* to describe the unicorn?

**6.** Why do you think the unicorn showed Rhiannon, and not the other villagers, where to dig for truffles?

**7.** When the trackers found Sir Brangwyn's body, it was "pierced through from side to side." How do you think he was killed?

## RESPONDING TO THE STORY

A "friendship" between an animal and a human is a common theme in art, literature, and film. Think of an example of such a friendship that you have either read about or seen in a movie or on television. Describe how the friendship was formed, why it was so strong, and what the outcome was.

## REVIEWING VOCABULARY

Match each word on the left with the correct definition on the right.

1. bellowing
2. cavorting
3. entranced
4. farthing
5. foal
6. heir
7. maiden

a. an unmarried girl or young woman
b. charmed; filled with delight
c. an old British coin with little value
d. a young horse
e. romping around happily
f. anyone who inherits money or property from a person who has died
g. calling out loudly; roaring

## THINKING CRITICALLY

1. Why do you think that the unicorn formed a bond with Rhiannon? Why did she, in turn, form a strong bond with the unicorn?
2. How do you think Rhiannon felt about the death of Sir Brangwyn? Support your conclusion by using details and examples from the story.
3. At the end of the story, Rhiannon said to her parents, "Unicorns have parents, too." What do you think she meant? How does this story show the power of love? Give details from the story to answer these questions.

# THOSE THREE WISHES

## A Wishful Cautionary Tale

### Judith Gorog

*It's your birthday. The cake is set down in front of you. Everyone urges: "Now make a wish and blow out the candles!" You squeeze your eyes shut and concentrate. What is it that you want more than anything else? a CD player? a pair of the most popular sneakers? You know that your wish won't necessarily come true. But wouldn't it be great if it did? Or would it?*

*What would happen if all our wishes did come true? Would we find out that our fulfilled wishes didn't make us as happy as we had thought they would? Could our fulfilled wishes backfire on us?*

*Is it really possible to change our destinies by making a wish? Perhaps we would learn, as Melinda Alice in this story learns, "Be careful what you wish for—it might come true!"*

## VOCABULARY WORDS

**witty** (WIHT-ee) clever and amusing
❖ We enjoy their company because they are so *witty*.

**malice** (MAL-ihs) desire to harm
❖ Many suffered from the king's *malice*.

**myopic** (my-OHP-ihk) nearsighted
❖ The *myopic* student couldn't see the blackboard.

**contamination** (kuhn-tam-uh-NAY-shuhn) impureness, pollution
❖ The *contamination* of the city's drinking water required everyone to buy bottled water.

**inoculated** (ih-NAHK-yoo-layt-uhd) introduced the germs of a disease to prevent that disease
❖ The children were *inoculated* against measles.

**scope** (skohp) range or opportunity for action
❖ The new job offered a greater *scope* for his abilities.

**retorted** (rih-TAWRT-uhd) replied quickly or sharply
❖ When I asked her to marry me, she *retorted*, "Never!"

**triumphantly** (try-UM-fuhnt-lee) in a way that shows success or victory
❖ After the championship game, the team waved *triumphantly* to the crowd.

**altruist** (AL-troo-ihst) an unselfish person
❖ The *altruist* gave all her money to a community center.

**grimaced** (grih-MAYST) made a face to show pain or disgust
❖ When she twisted her ankle, she *grimaced* in pain.

**N**o one ever said that Melinda Alice was nice. That wasn't the word used. No, she was clever, even witty. She was called— never to her face, however—Melinda Malice. Melinda Alice was clever and cruel. Her mother, when she thought about it at all, hoped Melinda would grow out of it. To her father, Melinda's very good grades mattered.

It was Melinda Alice, back in the eighth grade, who had labeled the shy, myopic new girl "Contamination" and was the first to pretend that anything or anyone touched by the new girl had to be cleaned, inoculated, or avoided. High school had merely given Melinda Alice greater scope for her talents.

The surprising thing about Melinda Alice was her power. No one trusted her, but no one avoided her either. She was always included, always in the middle. If you had seen her, pretty and witty, in the center of a group of students walking past your house, you'd have thought, "There goes a natural leader."

Melinda Alice had left for school early. She wanted to study alone in a quiet spot because there was going to be a big math test, and Melinda Alice was not pre- pared. That 'A' mattered, so Melinda Alice walked to school alone, planning her studies. She didn't usually notice nature much, so she nearly stepped on a beauti- ful snail that was making its way across the sidewalk.

"Ugh. Yucky thing," thought Melinda Alice. Not wanting to step on the snail accidentally was one thing, but now she lifted her shoe to crush it.

"Please don't," said the snail.

"Why not?" retorted Melinda Alice.

"I'll give you three wishes," replied the snail evenly.

"Agreed," said Melinda Alice. "My first wish is that

my next," she paused a split second, "my next thousand wishes come true." She smiled triumphantly and opened her bag to take out a small notebook and pencil to keep track.

Melinda Alice was sure she heard the snail say, "What a clever girl," as it made it to the safety of an ivy bed beside the sidewalk.

During the rest of the walk to school, Melinda was occupied with wonderful ideas. She would have beautiful clothes. "Wish number two, that I will always be perfectly dressed," and she was just that. True, her new outfit was not a lot different from the one she had worn leaving the house, but that only meant Melinda Alice liked her own taste.

After thinking awhile, she wrote, "Wish number three. I wish for pierced ears and small gold earrings."

Her father had not allowed Melinda to have pierced ears, but now she had them anyway. She felt her new earrings and shook her beautiful hair in delight. "I can have anything: stereo, tapes, TV, videodisk, moped, car, anything! All my life!" She hugged her books to herself in delight.

By the time she reached school, Melinda was almost an altruist. She could wish for peace. Then she wondered, "Is the snail that powerful?" She felt her ears, looked at her perfect blouse, skirt, jacket, shoes. "I could make ugly people beautiful, cure cripples . . ." She stopped. The wave of altruism had washed past. "I could pay people back who deserve it!" Melinda Alice looked at the school, at all the kids. She had an enormous sense of power. "They all have to do what I want now." She walked down the crowded halls to her locker. Melinda Alice could be sweet. She could be witty. She could—The bell rang for homeroom. Melinda Alice stashed her books, slammed the locker shut, and just made it to her seat.

"Hey, Melinda Alice," whispered Fred. "You know that big math test next period?"

"Oh, no" grimaced Melinda Alice. Her thoughts raced; "That snail made me late, and I forgot to study."

"I'll blow it," she groaned aloud. "I wish I were dead."

## READING FOR UNDERSTANDING

The following paragraph summarizes the story. Decide which of the words below the paragraph best fits in each blank. Two of the words are used twice. Write your answers on a separate sheet of paper.

Melinda Alice was **(1)**_____ and witty, but she also was **(2)**_____. Even though no one **(3)**_____ her, she was always **(4)**_____. One day as Melinda was walking to school, she almost stepped on a **(5)**_____. She thought it was **(6)**_____ and wanted to **(7)**_____ it. But the **(8)**_____ promised to give her **(9)**_____ **(10)**_____ if she would let it live. She agreed and her first **(11)**_____ was that her next **(12)**_____ wishes would come true. On the way to school, she wished for beautiful **(13)**_____ and gold **(14)**_____. But she also planned to use her power on the other **(15)**_____ at school. When she **(16)**_____ that she forgot to **(17)**_____ for the math test, she said, "I **(18)**_____ I were **(19)**_____."

**Words:**  *clever, clothes, cruel, crush, dead, disgusting, earrings, included, kids, realized, snail, study, thousand, three, trusted, wish, wishes*

## RESPONDING TO THE STORY

This story cautions against making foolish wishes. Quickly make a list of what you would wish for if you had three wishes. Then reread your list and think about the possible consequences of those wishes. What changes would you make to your list now?

## REVIEWING VOCABULARY

Match each word on the left with the correct definition on the right.

| | |
|---|---|
| **1.** altruist | **a.** made a face to show pain or disgust |
| **2.** contamination | |
| **3.** grimaced | **b.** nearsighted |
| **4.** inoculated | **c.** an unselfish person |
| **5.** myopic | **d.** clever and amusing |
| **6.** retorted | **e.** pollution |
| **7.** scope | **f.** in a way that shows success or victory |
| **8.** triumphantly | |
| **9.** witty | **g.** desire to harm |
| **10.** malice | **h.** room or opportunity for action |
| | **i.** replied quickly or sharply |
| | **j.** introduced germs of a disease to prevent that disease |

## THINKING CRITICALLY

**1.** Melinda obviously has some bad personality traits, yet she is a quick thinker and a born leader. What kinds of changes do you think she needs to make in order to put her traits to good use?

**2.** When you read Melinda's last wish, what was your reaction? Were you upset or secretly happy? Did you think that her last wish was funny? Did you think that the author wanted you to have that response? Explain why or why not, using examples from the story.

# HOW THE THREE YOUNG MEN FOUND DEATH

## adapted from a story by Geoffrey Chaucer

*Geoffrey Chaucer is considered the best English writer of the 14th century. He wrote about the people of his day, from the richest to the poorest. He had a gift for creating realistic characters, some of whom were quite unpleasant. In their efforts to get what they wanted, they often found themselves face to face with the unexpected.*

*You probably won't like the three young men in the story that you are about to read. They are bold and greedy. They gamble too much, and they drink too much. Although they are supposed to be friends, they do not trust one another.*

*Hoping to show how brave they are, these three men set out to find and conquer Death itself. While on their search for Death, they discover a way to get rich quick. They rejoice and give up their search. But Death lurks just around the corner. Read this story to find out how each of the three men meets up with Death in the final chilling scene.*

## VOCABULARY WORDS

**folly** (FAHL-ee) foolishness
❖ In the end, the men paid a high price for their *folly*.

**procession** (pruh-SEHSH-uhn) moving forward in a formal, orderly way
❖ The crowd grew quiet as the *procession* drew near.

**plague** (PLAYG) deadly epidemic disease
❖ During the Middle Ages, countless people died from outbreaks of *plague*.

**pact** (PAKT) agreement
❖ The three men made a *pact* to remain loyal to one another.

**shroud** (SHROWD) cloth used to wrap a corpse for burial
❖ The old man's extreme age, as well as the *shroud* that covered him, suggested a corpse.

**bushels** (BOOSH-uhlz) units of dry measure, each one equal to 32 quarts
❖ The crop was so good that we gave away *bushels* of apples.

**apothecary** (uh-PAHTH-uh-kehr-ee) druggist, pharmacist
❖ In medieval times, people obtained medicines and other healing drugs from the town *apothecary*.

## KEY WORD

**Flanders** (FLAN-duhrz) region in northwest Europe
❖ Much of *Flanders* lies in the country of Belgium.

 **In Flanders,** there was once a group of young men who devoted themselves to folly of all kinds: rioting, gambling, and drinking. They danced and played dice both day and night, and drank more than they should.

One day, as three of these young men sat in a tavern, they heard the clanging bell of a funeral procession. One of them called out to a young waiter, "Go and ask what corpse is passing by here."

"Why, sir," said the boy, "there is no need to ask. Someone told me only a short time ago. The dead man was a friend of yours. Last night, as he sat drinking on his bench, the thief that men call Death suddenly came by. With his spear, Death cut the man's heart in two and then went away without another word. He has taken thousands with his plague, and I would suggest that you be careful to avoid his presence."

The innkeeper then said: "The boy is telling the truth, for Death has taken many—men, women, and children—in the village this year. It seems as if he has made his home here."

"Is there such danger in meeting him?" one young man asked. "Why, then, I shall look for him in every street. Let the three of us make a pact. Let us hold up our hands and swear to be brothers and to find and kill this traitor who has killed so many others!" A traitor is a person who turns on others, and the three men vowed to stop this one.

So, together, these three made their pact: to live and die for one another as brothers. And they started off to find Death, shouting that Death was as good as dead, if only they could find him.

When they had gone less than half a mile, they came upon an old man who gave them a friendly greeting.

The proudest of the three young men said to the old man, "You scoundrel, why are you all covered except for your face? How have you lived to be so old?"

The old man answered, "Even if I were to walk as far as India, I would not be able to find a man who would be willing to trade his youth for my age. And, therefore, I shall keep my age for as long as I live. So I walk around the earth in my shroud, hoping for death to come and take me.

"None of you has manners. You should not speak so unkindly to an old man. You should treat an old man who has done you no harm as kindly as you would want to be treated in your old age—if you live so long. And now I must go."

"Oh, no, old dog," said the youth. "You shall not leave so easily. You just spoke now of the traitor Death, who has been killing all of our friends in this area. I think that you are his spy, and I demand that you tell me where he is. Surely you are one of his helpers who kill young people."

"Now, sirs," he said, "if you are so eager to find Death, turn up this crooked path. I left him under a tree in that grove, and there he will stay. Death will not hide from your boasting. Do you see that oak? You will find him there."

So, together, the three young men ran until they came to the tree. But there was no one there. Instead they found eight bushels of coins—round and shiny gold pieces. The sight of such wealth drove all thoughts of Death from their minds, and they sat down by their precious treasure.

"Brothers," said one, "listen closely to what I say. Fortune has given us this treasure, and we shall spend it as easily as we found it. Once this gold is carried away from this place, to my house or to yours—for we know that all this gold is ours—then all will be well. We shall spend the gold as we see fit.

But, after all, we cannot do it by daylight. Then people would say that we were thieves and hang us for our treasure. It must be carried away by night as carefully and secretly as we can. Therefore, let us draw lots to see which of us shall go into town to bring back food and drink. Then, when it is night, we shall carry it away to wherever we agree is the best place."

So, one man held three blades of grass in his closed hand. He who chose the shortest blade would have to go into town. The youngest of the three drew the shortest blade, and he went off toward the town. As soon as he was gone, one of the men said to the other, "You know that you are my sworn brother, and now I will tell you your reward. Our friend has gone into town, but here is the gold—and plenty of it!—to be divided among the three of us. But if I can help it, it shall only be divided between us two. Isn't this a great favor to do a friend?"

The other answered, "I don't know how that can be. What will we do? What will we say to him?"

"Will you keep it a secret?" asked the first man. "If so, I will tell you in a few words how we will bring it about."

"I promise, by my honor," said the other, "that I will not betray you."

"Now," said the first, "there are two of us, and two are stronger than one. When he comes back, watch when he sits down, and right away stand up as though you want to wrestle with him. While you struggle with him, as in sport, I will stab him through the side. Then, with your dagger, you do the same. And then, my dear friend, all this gold will be divided only between you and me. We can both have everything we want and

**110**

gamble as much as we like." And so these two agreed
to kill the third.

On his way into town, the youngest thought of nothing but the bright and shiny gold coins. He thought:
"If only I could have all that gold for myself. Then I
would be the happiest man in the world."

At last he decided that he would buy poison, with
which to kill his two partners. When he got into town,
he went straight to the apothecary and asked for poison to kill some rats.

The apothecary answered, "I will give you something that no living person or animal can withstand.
Once you have given it, the creature will be dead before
you have walked a mile—it is so strong and violent."

The young man took the box of poison. On the next

street, he met a man, from whom he bought three large bottles. He poured the poison into two and kept the third clean for his own drink. When he had filled the three bottles with wine, he returned to the tree where his friends waited for him.

Just as they had planned, the other two killed him as soon as he returned. And when they had done this, one said, "Let us sit down and drink and celebrate. We will bury him later." So he took one of the bottles with the poisoned wine and drank it down. Then he gave one of the other two bottles to his friend.

And soon, like their friend, the two found Death.

## READING FOR UNDERSTANDING

The following paragraph summarizes the story. Decide which of the words below the paragraph best fits in each blank. Write your answers on a separate sheet of paper.

Three young men sat in a **(1)**_____. When they heard the clanging **(2)**_____ of a funeral **(3)**_____, a boy told them that the corpse was one of their **(4)**_____. The young men made a **(5)**_____ always to be loyal to one another. They met an old **(6)**_____. He told them to look for Death under an **(7)**_____. There they found eight bushels of gold **(8)**_____ and decided to wait until **(9)**_____ to carry the gold away. While the youngest was away, the other two plotted to **(10)**_____ him. The youngest wanted all the gold for **(11)**_____. So he went straight to an **(12)**_____ and asked for **(13)**_____ to kill **(14)**_____. Then he bought three large **(15)**_____, filled two with poisoned wine, and returned to his companions. They killed him just as they had **(16)**_____, but after drinking the poisoned wine, they too found Death.

**Words:** *oak, kill, bell, poison, planned, rats, friends, procession, tavern, pact, bottles, apothecary, himself, man, night, coins*

## RESPONDING TO THE STORY

This story takes place hundreds of years ago. In what ways is the story still meaningful today? Explain your answer with examples from modern life.

## REVIEWING VOCABULARY

1. If people make a *pact*, they have an **(a)** objection **(b)** agreement **(c)** appointment.
2. You are a victim of *folly* if your behavior is **(a)** foolish **(b)** cautious **(c)** affectionate.
3. When a *plague* has broken out, **(a)** many people have celebrated **(b)** many people have died **(c)** many people have moved.
4. In a *procession* you will probably find people **(a)** eating **(b)** working **(c)** walking.
5. A purchase from an *apothecary* would most likely be **(a)** an item of clothing **(b)** a healing drug **(c)** a carpentry tool.
6. One place that you might see a *shroud* is at a **(a)** garden show **(b)** funeral **(c)** bank.

## THINKING CRITICALLY

1. This story suggests a close connection between the character flaws of the three young men and their violent fates. List some of the men's character flaws. Then explain in your own words how what finally happened to them is a direct result of these character flaws.
2. This story illustrates an old saying: "There is no honor among thieves." Explain what the saying means and how it relates to this story.
3. In this story, Death is **personified**. That means it is portrayed as if it were a person. Make a list of some of Death's "character traits," as they are described in the story.

# Unit 4

## TEMPTING FATE

# THE 11:59

## Patricia C. McKissack

*Have your grandparents or some other older persons ever told you about the "old days"? Stories of the way things used to be are often entertaining. They can make us feel happy, sad, or grateful. In fact, most of these stories make us feel glad that we have what we have today, thanks to those who came before us. Some of the things that we take for granted are things that another generation had to work and struggle for.*

*In the following story, you will meet Lester Simmons. He is a retired Pullman car porter. Lester is proud of the work he did, and the union he helped to form. The young porters owe a great deal to Lester's hard work and determination. They love Lester and the stories he tells. Read this story and find out if Lester's saddest story comes true.*

# VOCABULARY WORDS

**supplement** (SUP-luh-mehnt) add to; supply what is lacking
❖ I need to *supplement* my income by getting a second job.

**meager** (MEE-guhr) small in amount; inadequate
❖ My daughter feels that her allowance is *meager*.

**fledgling** (FLEHJ-lihng) young and inexperienced
❖ The *fledgling* baseball team hired new players.

**berths** (berths) built-in beds on a train or ship
❖ After a long day of travel, it felt good to lie in our *berths*.

**chided** (CHYD-id) mildly scolded
❖ She *chided* her son for eating the last piece of pie.

**mesmerizing** (MEHZ-muhr-y-zihng) fascinating
❖ The children loved their grandfather's *mesmerizing* tales of his life at sea.

**finery** (FYN-uhr-ee) showy clothes or jewelry
❖ Dressed in all her *finery*, she seemed to sparkle.

**restraint** (rih-STRAYNT) means of holding back or keeping down
❖ Use a *restraint* on that dog if it continues to bother people.

# KEY WORDS

**Pullman** (POOL-muhn) a railroad passenger car with convertible berths for sleeping
❖ I bought a *Pullman* train ticket for overnight travel.

**porter** (PAWR-tuhr) a person who carries luggage for hire
❖ We hired a *porter* to handle our luggage.

*From 1880 to 1960—a time known as the golden age of train travel—George Pullman's luxury sleeping cars provided passengers with comfortable accommodations during an overnight trip. The men who changed the riding seats into well-made-up beds and attended to the individual needs of each passenger were called Pullman car porters. For decades all the porters were African Americans, so when they organized the Brotherhood of Sleeping Car Porters in 1926, theirs was the first all-black union in the United States. Like most groups, the porters had their own language and a network of stories. The phantom Death Train, known in railroad language as the 11:59, is an example of the kind of story the porters often shared.*

Lester Simmons was a thirty-year retired Pullman car porter—had his gold watch to prove it. "Keeps perfect train time," he often bragged. "Good to the second."

Daily he went down to the St. Louis Union Station and shined shoes to help supplement his meager twenty-four-dollar-a-month Pullman retirement check. He ate his evening meal at the porter house on Compton Avenue and hung around until late at night talking union, playing bid whist, and spinning yarns with those who were still "travelin' men." In this way Lester stayed in touch with the only family he'd known since 1920.

There was nothing the young porters liked more than listening to Lester tell true stories about the old days, during the founding of the Brotherhood of Sleeping Car Porters, the first black union in the United States. He knew the president, A. Philip Randolph, personally, and proudly boasted that it was

Randolph who'd signed him up as a union man back in 1926. He passed his original card around for inspection. "I knew all the founding brothers. Take Brother E. J. Bradley. We hunted many a day together, not for the sport of it but for something to eat. Those were hard times, starting up the union. But we hung in there so you youngsters might have the benefits you enjoy now."

The rookie porters always liked hearing about the thirteen-year struggle between the Brotherhood and the powerful Pullman Company, and how, against all odds, the fledgling union had won recognition and better working conditions.

Everybody enjoyed it too when Lester told tall tales about Daddy Joe, the porters' larger-than-life hero. "Now, y'all know the first thing a good Pullman man is expected to do is make up the top and lower berths for the passengers each night."

"Come on, Lester," one of his listeners chided. "You don't need to describe our jobs for us."

"Some of you, maybe not. But some of you, well—" he said, looking over the top of his glasses and raising an eyebrow at a few of the younger porters. "I was just setting the stage." He smiled good-naturedly and went on with his story. "They tell me Daddy Joe could walk flat-footed down the center of the coach and let down berths on both sides of the aisle."

Hearty laughter filled the room, because everyone knew that to accomplish such a feat, Daddy Joe would have to have been superhuman. But that was it: To the men who worked the sleeping cars, Daddy Joe was no less a hero than Paul Bunyan was to the lumberjacks of the Northwestern forests.

"And when the 11:59 pulled up to his door, as big and strong as Daddy Joe was . . ." Lester continued solemnly. "Well, in the end even he couldn't escape the

11:59." The old storyteller eyed one of the rookie porters he knew had never heard the frightening tale about the porters' Death Train. Lester took joy in mesmerizing his young listeners with all the details.

"Any porter who hears the whistle of the 11:59 has got exactly twenty-four hours to clear up earthly matters. He better be ready when the train comes the next night . . ." In his creakiest voice, Lester drove home the point: "All us porters got to board that train one day. Ain't no way to escape the final ride on the 11:59."

*Silence.*

"Lester," a young porter asked, "you know anybody who ever heard the whistle of the 11:59 and lived to tell—"

"Not a living soul!"

*Laughter.*

"Well," began one of the men, "wonder who will have to make up berths on *that* train?"

"If it's an overnight trip to heaven, you can best be believing there's bound to be a few of us making up the berths," another answered.

"Shucks," a card player stopped to put in. "They say even up in heaven *we* the ones gon' be keeping all that gold and silver polished."

"Speaking of gold and silver," Lester said, remembering. "That reminds me of how I gave Tip Sampson his nickname. Y'all know Tip?"

There were plenty of nods and smiles.

The memory made Lester chuckle. He shifted in his seat to find a more comfortable spot. Then he began. "A woman got on board the *Silver Arrow* in Chicago going to Los Angeles. She was dripping in finery—had on all kinds of gold and diamond jewelry, carried twelve bags. Sampson knocked me down getting to wait on her, figuring she was sure for a big tip. That lady was worrisome! Ooowee! 'Come do this. Go do that. Bring me this.' Sampson was running over himself trying to keep that lady happy. When we reached L.A., my passengers all tipped me two or three dollars, as was customary back then.

When Sampson's Big Money lady got off, she reached into her purse and placed a dime in his outstretched hand. A *dime*! Can you imagine? *Ow*! You should have seen his face. And I didn't make it no better. Never did let him forget it. I teased him so—went to calling him Tip, and the nickname stuck."

*Laughter.*

"I haven't heard from ol' Tip in a while. Anybody know anything?"

"You haven't got word, Lester? Tip boarded the 11:59 over in Kansas City about a month ago."

"Sorry to hear that. That just leaves me and Willie Beavers, the last of the old, old-timers here in St. Louis."

Lester looked at his watch—it was a little before midnight. The talkfest had lasted later than usual. He said his good-byes and left, taking his usual route across the Eighteenth Street bridge behind the station.

In the darkness, Lester looked over the yard, picking out familiar shapes—the *Hummingbird*, the *Zephyr*. He'd worked on them both. Train travel wasn't anything like it used to be in the old days—not since people had begun to ride airplanes. "Progress," he scoffed. "Those contraptions will never take the place of a train. No sir!"

Suddenly he felt a sharp pain in his chest. At exactly the same moment he heard the mournful sound of a train whistle, which the wind seemed to carry from some faraway place. Ignoring his pain, Lester looked at the old station. He knew nothing was scheduled to

**121**

come in or out till early morning. Nervously he lit a match to check the time. 11:59!

"No," he said into the darkness. "I'm not ready. I've got plenty of living yet."

Fear quickened his step. Reaching his small apartment, he hurried up the steps. His heart pounded in his ear, and his left arm tingled. He had an idea, and there wasn't a moment to waste. But his own words haunted him. *Ain't no way to escape the final ride on the 11:59.*

"But I'm gon' try!" Lester spent the rest of the night plotting his escape from fate.

"I won't eat or drink anything all day," he talked himself through his plan. "That way I can't choke, die of food poisoning, or cause a cooking fire."

Lester shut off the space heater to avoid an explosion, nailed shut all doors and windows to keep out intruders, and unplugged every electrical appliance. Good weather was predicted, but just in case a freak storm came and blew out a window, shooting deadly glass shards in his direction, he moved a straight-backed chair into a far corner, making sure nothing was overhead to fall on him.

"I'll survive," he said, smiling at the prospect of beating Death. "Won't that be a wonderful story to tell at the porter house?" He rubbed his left arm. It felt numb again.

Lester sat silently in his chair all day, too afraid to move. At noon someone knocked on his door. He couldn't answer it. Footsteps . . . another knock. He didn't answer.

A parade of minutes passed by, equally measured, one behind the other, ticking . . . ticking . . . away . . . The dull pain in his chest returned. He nervously checked his watch every few minutes.

*Ticktock, ticktock.*

**122**

Time had always been on his side. Now it was his enemy. Where had the years gone? Lester reviewed the thirty years he'd spent riding the rails. How different would his life have been if he'd married Louise Henderson and had a gallon of children? What if he'd taken that job at the mill down in Opelika? What if he'd followed his brother to Philly? How different?

*Ticktock, ticktock.*

So much living had passed so quickly. Lester decided if he had to do it all over again, he'd stand by his choices. His had been a good life. No regrets. No major changes for him.

*Ticktock, ticktock.*

The times he'd had—both good and bad—what memories. His first and only love had been traveling, and she was a jealous companion. Wonder whatever happened to that girl up in Minneapolis? Thinking about her made him smile. Then he laughed. That girl must be close to seventy years old by now.

*Ticktock, ticktock.*

Daylight was fading quickly. Lester drifted off to sleep, then woke from a nightmare in which, like Jonah, he'd been swallowed by an enormous beast. Even awake he could still hear its heart beating . . . *ticktock, ticktock* . . . But then he realized he was hearing his own heartbeat.

Lester couldn't see his watch, but he guessed no more than half an hour had passed. Sleep had overtaken him with such little resistance. Would Death, that shapeless shadow, slip in that easily? Where was he lurking? *Yea, though I walk through the valley of the shadow of death, I will fear no evil* . . . The Twenty-third Psalm was the only prayer Lester knew, and he repeated it over and over, hoping it would comfort him.

Lester rubbed his tingling arm. He could hear the

blood rushing past his ear and up the side of his head. He longed to know what time it was, but that meant he had to light a match—too risky. What if there was a gas leak? The match would set off an explosion. "I'm too smart for that, Death," he said.

*Ticktock, ticktock.*

It was late. He could feel it. Stiffness seized his legs and made them tremble. How much longer? he wondered. Was he close to winning?

Then in the fearful silence he heard a train whistle. His ears strained to identify the sound, making sure it *was* a whistle. No mistake. It came again, the same as the night before. Lester answered it with a groan.

*Ticktock, ticktock.*

He could hear time ticking away in his head. Gas leak or not, he had to see his watch. Striking a match, Lester quickly checked the time. 11:57.

Although there was no gas explosion, a tiny explosion erupted in his heart.

*Ticktock, ticktock.*

Just a little more time. The whistle sounded again. Closer than before. Lester struggled to move, but he felt fastened to the chair. Now he could hear the engine puffing, pulling a heavy load. It was hard for him to breathe, too, and the pain in his chest weighed heavier and heavier.

*Ticktock, ticktock.*

Time had run out! Lester's mind reached for an explanation that made sense. But reason failed when a glowing phantom dressed in the porters' blue uniform stepped out of the grayness of Lester's confusion.

"It's *your* time, good brother." The specter spoke in a thousand familiar voices.

Freed of any restraint now, Lester stood, bathed in a peaceful calm that had its own glow. "Is that you, Tip?"

he asked, squinting to focus on his old friend standing in the strange light.

"It's me, ol' partner. Come to remind you that none of us can escape the last ride on the 11:59."

"I know, I know," Lester said, chuckling. "But man, I had to try."

Tip smiled. "I can dig it. So did I."

"That'll just leave Willie, won't it?"

"Not for long."

"I'm ready."

Lester saw the great beam of the single headlight and heard the deafening whistle blast one last time before the engine tore through the front of the apartment, shattering glass and splintering wood, collapsing everything in its path, including Lester's heart.

When Lester didn't show up at the shoeshine stand two days running, friends went over to his place and found him on the floor. His eyes were fixed on something quite amazing—his gold watch, stopped at exactly 11:59.

## READING FOR UNDERSTANDING

**1.** What is the 11:59? What happens if you hear its whistle?
**2.** Why did all the porters enjoy listening to Lester's stories?
**3.** How did Tip Sampson get his nickname?
**4.** What type of person was Sampson's Big Money lady?
**5.** What did Lester do to try to escape the 11:59? Did it buy him more time? How do you know?
**6.** How did Lester's feelings about the 11:59 change by the end of the story?
**7.** What was the author's purpose in repeating *"Ticktock, ticktock"* throughout the second half of the story?

## RESPONDING TO THE STORY

What were your feelings as you read the story? Did they change at the end of the story? What parts of the story stood out in your mind? Write a paragraph summarizing your feelings about Lester and the 11:59.

## REVIEWING VOCABULARY

**1.** Travelers use *berths* if **(a)** they have a lot of luggage **(b)** the climate is cold **(c)** they are traveling overnight.
**2.** I *chided* her because she **(a)** bought me a present **(b)** told me the correct time **(c)** forgot to call me.
**3.** You would most likely see *finery* **(a)** at a party **(b)** in the library **(c)** on the beach.
**4.** A *fledgling* actor **(a)** is just starting out **(b)** has many offers for parts **(c)** does only comedy.

**5.** If you received a *meager* raise, you would probably **(a)** celebrate **(b)** feel upset **(c)** be satisfied.

**6.** Someone who tells *mesmerizing* stories **(a)** bores people **(b)** embarrasses people **(c)** fascinates people.

**7.** An example of a *restraint* is a **(a)** seat belt **(b)** tire **(c)** train.

## THINKING CRITICALLY

**1.** Lester tells his friends, "Ain't no way to escape the final ride on the 11:59." However, when the 11:59 comes for Lester, he tries to escape it. Why do you think he did so? Use details from the story to support your response.

**2.** Do you like the character of Lester? Why or why not? You might want to consider his relationships and his life choices.

**3.** What kinds of stories do you think Lester's friends will be telling about him? Use details from the story to write some story suggestions.

**127**

# THE ADVENTURE OF THE SPECKLED BAND

## adapted from a story by Arthur Conan Doyle

*Do you enjoy mysteries? Do you like detective stories? Then the Sherlock Holmes stories are for you. Written by Arthur Conan Doyle, the 19th century English writer, these are some of the best detective mysteries we have. They have delighted millions of readers over the years. Many of these stories have even been made into movies.*

*Sherlock Holmes is Conan Doyle's brilliant detective. Holmes is famous for never losing his cool and always solving the crime. His assistant, Doctor Watson, is the one who tells the reader all about each case.*

*There is always an exciting twist to each Sherlock Holmes tale. Few readers can guess how the crime will be solved until the very last page. In "The Adventure of the Speckled Band," a frightened woman comes to Holmes and Watson with a very peculiar story. As you read, play the part of a detective on the case. Can you solve the mystery of the speckled band?*

## VOCABULARY WORDS

**speckled** (SPEHK-uhld) covered with small marks
❖ The car tire was *speckled* with dried mud.

**intimate** (IHN-tuh-muht) very close
❖ My cousin and I became *intimate* friends over the summer.

**fatal** (FAYT-uhl) leading to death or ruin
❖ Unfortunately, the car accident was *fatal*.

**writhed** (RYTHD) twisted and turned
❖ The snake *writhed* across the lawn.

**coroner** (KAWR-uh-nuhr) medical examiner of the dead
❖ The *coroner* stated that the man had died of food poisoning.

**delirium** (dih-LIHR-ee-uhm) state of overexcitement or insanity
❖ The fever caused him to fall into a *delirium*.

**imperturbably** (ihm-puhr-TER-buh-blee) very calmly
❖ Though I was late, I *imperturbably* took a long bath.

**vigil** (VIHJ-uhl) staying up at night to keep watch
❖ They held a *vigil* over the sick person until dawn.

## KEY WORDS

**Surrey** (SUHR-ee) a county to the southwest of London
❖ She worked in London but spent her weekends in *Surrey*.

**bell-rope** (BEHL ROHP) rope used to ring a bell for a servant
❖ As soon as she pulled the *bell-rope*, a servant appeared.

 **Of all the varied cases** I have solved with my friend Sherlock Holmes, I cannot recall any stranger than that of the well-known Roylott family. It was early in April in the year 1883, when I woke one morning to find Sherlock Holmes standing by the side of my bed.

"Very sorry to wake you up, Watson," said he. "A young lady has arrived in a considerable state of excitement and is waiting in the sitting room."

I threw on my clothes and was ready in a few minutes. A lady, dressed in black and heavily veiled, was sitting at the window.

"Good morning, madam," said Holmes cheerily. "My name is Sherlock Holmes, and this is my intimate friend and associate, Dr. Watson. You can speak freely before him. I shall order you a cup of hot coffee, for I observe that you are shivering."

"It is not cold that makes me shiver," said the woman in a low voice. "It is fear, Mr. Holmes."

She raised her veil as she spoke. Her face was drawn and gray, with restless, frightened eyes. Her features and figure were those of a woman of thirty, but her hair was prematurely gray. Sherlock Holmes observed her closely with one of his quick, all-knowing glances.

"You must not fear," he said soothingly, bending forward and patting her forearm. "We shall soon set matters right."

"Sir, I can stand this strain no longer. I have no one to turn to—except one who cares for me, and he can be of little aid. I have heard of you, Mr. Holmes. Oh, sir, do you think that you could help me, too? In a month or six weeks, I shall be married, with my own income, and then you shall not find me ungrateful."

Holmes answered, "My profession is its own reward.

**130**

And now, I beg you to tell us everything."

"Alas!" replied our visitor. "My fears are so vague that even my fiancé looks upon what I tell him as the fancies of a nervous woman."

"Go on, madam."

"My name is Helen Stoner, and I am living with my stepfather, Dr. Roylott, who is the last survivor of one of the oldest families in England."

Holmes nodded his head. "The name is familiar to me."

"The Roylott family was at one time among the richest in England. The family was eventually ruined by a gambler in the last century until nothing was left except a few acres of land. My stepfather borrowed money and earned a medical degree. He then traveled to Calcutta, India and established a large practice.

"When Dr. Roylott was in India, he married my mother, Mrs. Stoner, a widow. My twin sister Julia and I were only two years old at the time. My mother had a considerable sum of money—at least 1,000 pounds a year—which she bequeathed to Dr. Roylott. But a certain annual sum would be given to each of us in the event of our marriage. Shortly after our return to England, my mother was killed in a railway accident, and Dr. Roylott took us to live with him in his ancestral house at Stoke Moran.

"A terrible change came over our stepfather about this time. Instead of making friends with our neighbors, he shut himself up in his house and seldom came out except for ferocious quarrels with anyone who crossed his path.

"My stepfather has almost no friends. He only has a passion for animals from India, which are sent over to him. He now has a cheetah and a baboon that wander freely over his grounds and are feared by the villagers.

**131**

"My poor sister Julia and I had no great pleasure in our lives. No servant would stay with us, so we did all the work of the house. She was only thirty at the time of her death, but her hair had already begun to whiten, like mine."

"Your sister is dead, then?"

"She died just two years ago. It is of her death that I wish to speak to you. My sister Julia met a marine major, to whom she became engaged. My stepfather learned of the engagement and offered no objection to the marriage. But two weeks before the wedding, the terrible event occurred."

"Please be precise as to details," said Holmes.

"It is easy for me to be precise because every event of that dreadful time is seared into my memory. The manor house is very old, and only one wing has been inhabited. These bedrooms in this wing are on the ground floor. Of these bedrooms, the first is Dr. Roylott's, the second was my sister's, and the third is my own. The bedrooms are not connected to each other, but they all open out into the same corridor. Do I make myself clear?"

"Perfectly so."

"The windows of the three bedrooms open out onto the lawn.  Dr. Roylott had gone to his room early that fatal night. Before going to sleep, my sister left her room and came into mine. At eleven o'clock, she rose to leave, but she paused at the door."

"'Tell me, Helen,' she said, 'have you ever heard anyone whistle in the dead of the night?'"

"'Never,' said I. 'Why?'"

"'Because for the last few nights, I have always heard a low, clear whistle, at about three in the morning. I cannot tell where it comes from, so I thought that I would ask you whether you had heard it.'"

**132**

"'No, I have not.'"

"'I wonder why you did not hear it also.'"

"'Ah, but I sleep more heavily than you.'"

"'Well, it is of no great consequence, at any rate.'"
She smiled back at me and closed my door. A few
moments later, I heard her key turn in the lock."

"Indeed," said Holmes. "Was it your custom always
to lock yourselves in at night?"

"Always. I think that I mentioned to you that the
doctor kept a cheetah and a baboon on the grounds.
We didn't feel safe unless our doors were locked."

"Quite so. Please go on."

"I could not sleep that night because I had a feeling
of impending danger. Suddenly, I heard the wild
scream of a terrified woman and knew that it was my
sister's voice. I sprang from my bed and rushed into the
corridor. As I opened my door, I seemed to hear a low
whistle like the one that my sister described. I ran
down the hallway to find that my sister's door was
unlocked and swinging slowly upon its hinges. I saw
my sister appear in the doorway, her face white with
terror and her hands groping for help. Her whole figure swayed to and fro like that of a drunkard. At that
moment, her knees gave way, and she fell to the
ground, writhing as one who is in terrible pain. As I
bent over her, she suddenly shrieked out in a voice that
I shall never forget: 'Oh, my God! Helen! It was the
band! The speckled band!' She pointed her finger in the
direction of Doctor Roylott's room. I rushed out, calling
loudly for our stepfather, whom I met hastening from
his room in his dressing-gown. When he reached my
sister's side, she was already unconscious. She slowly
sank and died."

"One moment," said Holmes, "are you sure about
the whistle?"

"It is my strong impression that I heard it. Yet, between the blowing wind and the creaking of an old house, I may have been deceived."

"What conclusions did the coroner come to?"

"He was unable to find any satisfactory cause of death. The door to Julia's room had been fastened from the inside, and the windows were blocked by old-fashioned shutters with broad iron bars. It is certain that my sister was quite alone when she met her end. Besides, there were no marks of any violence upon her body."

"How about poison?"

"The doctors examined her for it, but without success. It is my belief that she died of pure fear and nervous shock. I cannot imagine what could have frightened her to death."

"Ah, and what do you think this speckled band is?"

"Sometimes I have thought that it was merely the wild talk of delirium. At other times, I have thought that a person wearing a speckled band or handkerchief killed Julia."

Holmes shook his head like a man who was far from being satisfied.

"Go on," he said.

"Two years have passed since then. My life has been lonelier than ever. However, a month ago, a dear friend asked for my hand in marriage. My stepfather has offered no opposition to the match, and we will be married in the spring. Two days ago, some repairs were started in the west wing of the house. My bedroom wall has been pierced, and I have had to move into the chamber in which my sister died. Imagine my terror when, last night, I suddenly heard the very same low whistle."

"Have you told me all?" asked Holmes.

"Yes, all."

"Miss Stoner, you have not. You are protecting your stepfather." Holmes pushed back the black lace around her wrist. Five red marks in the shape of four fingers and a thumb were imprinted upon the white wrist.

"You have been cruelly treated," said Holmes.

The lady blushed and covered her injured wrist. "He is a hard man," she said. "Perhaps he hardly knows his own strength."

"This is a strange business," said Holmes. "There are a thousand details that I need to know. Could we come to Stoke Moran today and see the rooms without the knowledge of your stepfather?"

"He said that he was going to town today on important business. He will probably be away all day."

"Excellent. Watson and I shall both come. You may expect us early in the afternoon."

"My heart has lightened since I have confided in you," said she, dropping her thick black veil over her face and gliding from the room.

"And what do you think of it all, Watson?" asked Sherlock Holmes, leaning back in his chair.

"It seems to me to be a most dark and sinister business."

"Yet, if the flooring and walls are sound, and the door and window and chimney are impassable, her sister must have been alone when she met her mysterious end."

"What about those whistles? And what about the very peculiar words of the dying woman?"

"I don't know."

"When you combine those whistles, the mention of a speckled band, and the stepfather's motive for preventing the marriage, I think that there is good ground to think that the mystery may be cleared."

"How can these clear it up?"

"I cannot imagine. That is why we are going to Stoke Moran."

Suddenly, our door was kicked open, revealing a huge man. He swung a hunting crop in his hand. So tall was he that his hat actually brushed the top of the doorway. His deep-set, yellowish eyes and his thin nose made him look like a fierce old bird of prey.

"Which of you is Holmes?" he demanded. "I am Dr. Grimesby Roylott."

"Indeed, Doctor," said Holmes blandly. "Please take a seat."

"I will do nothing of the kind. My stepdaughter has been here. I have followed her. What has she been saying to you?"

"It is a little cold for this time of the year," said Holmes.

"What has she been saying to you?" screamed the old man furiously.

"But I have heard that the crocuses should do well," continued my companion imperturbably.

"Ha! You put me off, do you?" said our new visitor, taking a step forward and shaking his hunting crop. "I know you, you meddler!"

My friend smiled.

"Holmes, the busybody!"

Holmes chuckled heartily. "Your conversation is most entertaining," said he. "When you go out, please close the door, as there is quite a draft."

"I will go when I have said my say. Don't you dare meddle with my affairs. I know that Miss Stoner has been here. I can be a dangerous man!" He seized the fireplace poker and bent it into a curve with his huge brown hands.

"See that you keep yourself out of my grip!" he

**136**

snarled. He hurled the twisted poker into the fireplace and strode out of the room.

"What a likable person," said Holmes, laughing. "I am not quite so bulky, but my grip is almost as strong as his own." He picked up the steel poker and, with a sudden effort, straightened it out again.

"And now, Watson, we shall order breakfast. Afterwards, I shall walk down to Doctors' Commons, where I hope to get some information."

It was nearly one o'clock when Sherlock Holmes returned. "I have seen the will of his dead wife," he said. "It is clear that if both girls had married, he would have received very little money. And now, Watson, we shall take a train to Surrey and then drive to Stoke Moran. Please slip your revolver into your pocket. That and a toothbrush are, I think, all that we need."

Nearing Stoke Moran, we drove for four or five miles through the lovely Surrey lanes. "There's the village," said the driver, pointing to some roofs to the left. "If you want to get to the Stoke Moran house, take the footpath over the fields where the lady is walking."

"And the lady, I fancy, is Miss Stoner," observed Holmes.

We got off and paid our fare. We called out to Miss Stoner. "Good afternoon, Miss Stoner. You see that we have been as good as our word."

"I have been waiting so eagerly for you," she cried. "Dr. Roylott is still in town."

"We have had the pleasure of making the doctor's acquaintance," said Holmes. He told what had occurred, and Miss Stoner turned white as she listened.

"He is so cunning that I never know when I am safe from him," she said.

"You must lock yourself up from him tonight. If he

is violent, we shall take you away to your aunt's at Harrow. Now kindly take us at once to the bedrooms."

The building was of gray stone, with a high central part and two curving wings, like the claws of a crab. In the left wing, the windows were broken and blocked with wooden boards, but the right-hand wing was comparatively modern. This was where the family lived. The stonework had been broken into, but there were no signs of any workmen now. Holmes walked slowly up and down the lawn and examined the outsides of the windows.

"This window belongs to the room in which you used to sleep. The middle window belongs to your sister's room. The one next to the main building belongs to Dr. Roylott's chamber?"

"Exactly. But now I am sleeping in the middle room."

"By the way, there does not seem to be any great need for repairs at that end wall."

"There were none. I think it was an excuse to move me from my room."

"Ah! Perhaps. Now, on the other side of this narrow wing runs the corridor from which these three rooms open?"

"Yes."

"You both locked your doors at night, so no one could enter your rooms from that side. Now, would you please go into your room and bar your shutters?"

Miss Stoner did so. Holmes tried to force the shutter open but without success. "No one could pass through these shutters if they were bolted, he exclaimed."

A small side door led into the corridor. Holmes examined the second bedroom, in which Miss Stoner's sister had met with her fate. His eyes traveled round and round in the room.

**138**

"Where does that bell ring?" he asked, pointing to a thick bell-rope that hung down beside the bed.

"In the housekeeper's room."

"It looks newer than the other things."

"Yes, it was only put there a couple of years ago."

Holmes took the bell-rope in his hand and gave it a brisk tug. "Why, it's a dummy," said he. "It is not even attached to the wire. It is fastened to a hook just above the little opening for the ventilator."

"How very absurd! I never noticed that before."

"Very strange!" muttered Holmes. "There are other strange things about this room. For example, why would a builder open a ventilator to your stepfather's room? With the same trouble, he might have built it to face the outside air! Was the ventilator put in at the

**139**

same time as the bell-rope?"

"Yes," said Miss Stoner.

We went immediately to Dr. Grimesby Roylott's bed-room. A large iron safe caught our interest.

"What's in here?" Holmes asked, tapping the safe. "There isn't a cat in it, for example?"

"No. What a strange idea!"

"Well, look at this!" He picked up a small saucer of milk that rested on top of the safe.

"No, we don't keep a cat. But there is a cheetah and a baboon."

"Ah, yes, of course! Well, a cheetah is just a big cat, and yet a saucer of milk does not go very far in satisfying its needs. But here is something interesting!"

There was a small whip hung on one corner of the bed. The end of the whip was tied to make a small loop.

"What do you make of that, Watson?"

"It's common enough, but I don't know why it should be tied."

I had never seen my friend's face so grim or his brow so dark. "Miss Stoner," said he, "both my friend and I must spend the night in your room." Both Miss Stoner and I stared at him in astonishment.

"You must stay in your room, pretending to have a headache, when your stepfather comes back. When he retires for the night, you must open your window shutters and quietly move into the room in which you used to sleep."

"But what will you do?" she asked.

"We shall spend the night in your room and investigate the cause of this noise that disturbed you."

Holmes and I then left Miss Stoner and waited at a nearby inn. At the stroke of eleven, a single bright light shone from a window of the manor house.

"That is our signal," said Holmes, springing to his feet. "It comes from the middle window."

A moment later, we were out on the dark lawn, a chill wind blowing in our faces. We were about to enter through the window when a hideous creature leaped out of some bushes and threw itself upon the grass.

"This is quite a household," Holmes murmured. "That is the baboon."

I had forgotten the strange pets. There was a cheetah, too. Perhaps it would land on our shoulders at any moment. I felt easier in my mind when I found myself inside the bedroom. My companion noiselessly closed the shutters.

He whispered into my ear. "The least sound would be fatal to our plans."

I nodded to show that I had heard.

"We must sit without light. He would see any light through the ventilator."

I nodded again.

"Do not fall asleep because your very life may depend upon it! Have your pistol ready in case we should need it. I will sit on the side of the bed, and you in that chair."

I took out my revolver and laid it on the corner of the table. Holmes had brought a long, thin cane, which he placed upon the bed beside him. He laid out a box of matches and the stump of a candle. Then he put out the lamp.

How shall I ever forget that dreadful, dark vigil? I could not hear a sound, not even the drawing of a breath.

Suddenly, there was a gleam of light coming from the ventilator, but it vanished almost immediately. Then all at once we heard another sound. It was like a small jet of steam escaping from a kettle. Holmes sprang from the bed! He struck a match and lashed furiously with his cane at the bell-rope!

"You see it, Watson?" he yelled. "You see it?"

But I saw nothing. At the moment when Holmes struck the match, I heard only a low, clear whistle. I could see that Holmes's face was deadly pale and filled with horror and loathing.

He had stopped hitting the bell-rope and was gazing up at the ventilator. Suddenly, the most horrible cry broke the silence of the night! It was a hoarse cry of pain and fear and anger, all mingled in one dreadful shriek.

"What can it mean?" I gasped.

"It means that it is all over," Holmes responded. "Take your pistol, and we will enter Dr. Roylott's room."

With a grave face, he lit the lamp and led the way down the corridor. Then he turned the handle, and we entered. On a chair sat Dr. Grimesby Roylott in a long, gray dressing gown. Across his lap lay the whip with the looped end that we had noticed during the day. His head was thrown back, and his eyes were fixed in a dreadful stare. Round his brow he had a peculiar yellow band with brownish speckles.

"The band! The speckled band!" whispered Holmes.

I took a step forward. In an instant, his strange headgear began to move. I made out the squat, diamond-shaped head and puffed neck of a loathsome snake.

"It is a swamp adder!" shouted Holmes. "The deadliest snake in India. He died within ten seconds of being bitten."

As he spoke, he drew the whip swiftly from the dead man's lap. Throwing the noose around the snake's neck, he then carried the snake at arm's length and threw it into the iron safe, which stood open.

**142**

Such are the true facts of the death of Dr. Grimesby Roylott of Stoke Moran. The doctor was bitten by his own snake. He had sent it through the ventilator to kill his stepdaughter, in the same way that he had killed her sister. But Holmes drove it back through the ventilator. The snake became so frightened that it bit Dr. Roylott.

In this way, Sherlock Holmes was responsible for Dr. Grimesby Roylott's death. I cannot say that it is likely to weigh very heavily upon his conscience.

# READING FOR UNDERSTANDING

1. Why do you think that Helen Stoner was heavily veiled when she came to see Holmes and Watson?
2. What sound did Helen Stoner's sister hear on the night that she died?
3. What reason did Dr. Roylott have for keeping his stepdaughters from getting married?
4. What did Dr. Roylott do to prove his strength to Holmes?
5. Why did Holmes think that Helen Stoner's sister might have died from poison?
6. Why did Holmes lash at the bell-rope with his cane?
7. How did Dr. Roylott die?

## RESPONDING TO THE STORY

Helen Stoner turned to Sherlock Holmes because even her fiancé would not listen to her fears. Have you ever been concerned about something that no one else took seriously? What was the result? Did your fears prove to be true, or were others right in telling you not to worry? Describe your experiences in the form of a journal entry.

## REVIEWING VOCABULARY

Match each word on the left with the correct definition on the right.

| | | | |
|---|---|---|---|
| **1.** vigil | | **a.** covered with small marks |
| **2.** fatal | | **b.** very close |
| **3.** delirium | | **c.** leading to death or ruin |
| **4.** speckled | | **d.** twisted and turned |
| **5.** coroner | | **e.** medical examiner of the dead |
| **6.** intimate | | **f.** state of overexcitement or insanity |
| **7.** writhed | | **g.** very calmly |
| **8.** imperturbably | | **h.** staying up at night to keep watch |

## THINKING CRITICALLY

**1.** What do you think of the way that Holmes treated Dr. Roylott when he burst into Holmes's room? Was it wise for Holmes to respond in such a cool and sarcastic manner? Why or why not?

**2.** Imagine that this story was rewritten from the point of view of Dr. Roylott. How might he explain his behavior? What is there about his past that made him so bitter?

**3.** Why do you think that Arthur Conan Doyle always has Dr. Watson tell us the story? How would it sound if Holmes were to describe his brilliant solution to a crime? Would that increase or decrease your enjoyment of the story?

# SISTER DEATH AND THE HEALER

## Robert D. Sans Souci

*There are many symbols for death in art, literature, and film. Angels and skeletons are figures that are often used to express the idea of death. In this story, Death is a skeletal figure in a cowl, driving a wooden cart.*

*Many people react with horror at the thought of death. But one of the characters in this story, José, is respectful and friendly when he comes face to face with Death. After all, according to José, Death does not discriminate. She takes both the rich and the poor, the weak and the powerful.*

*Because José seems to appreciate Death, she blesses him with a special power. But the power that he receives from her has one important condition. Read the story to find out what happens to José when he disregards that condition.*

# VOCABULARY WORDS

**readily** (REHD-uh-lee) willingly; quickly
❖ When he suggested that we go to the movies, I *readily* agreed.

**astounded** (uh-STOWN-duhd) greatly amazed
❖ We were *astounded* when they told us the price of their new house.

**ailing** (AYL-ihng) in poor health; sickly
❖ My *ailing* uncle did not have much longer to live.

**summoned** (SUM-uhnd) ordered to come; sent for
❖ The boss *summoned* everyone into her office.

**cowl** (KOWL) a monk's cloak and hood
❖ Because of the *cowl*, I could barely see her face.

**consequences** (KAHN-sih-kwehn-suhs) results of one's actions
❖ If you forget to study for the important exam, you will have to face the *consequences*.

**extinguished** (ihk-STIHN-gwihsht) put out; caused to die out
❖ The campers *extinguished* their fire before moving on.

# KEY WORD

**Señor** (seh-NYAWR) and **Señora** (seh-NYAW-rah) Spanish for "Mr." and "Mrs."
❖ *Señor* and *Señora* Rodriguez are coming from Puerto Rico to visit us.

**T**here **was once a woodcutter, José,** who fell asleep in the wood and did not wake until after dark. When he did, he met the skeletal figure of Manita Muerte, Sister Death, driving her wooden cart in which she gathers the souls of the newly departed.

"*Buenas noches, señora,*" said the woodcutter respectfully, recognizing the figure who stood before him.

"*Buenas noches, señor,*" Death replied. "Will you give me something to eat? The night is long, and I have grown hungry."

"*Sí, sí!*" said the woodcutter. He gave half of his rice and beans to her. "I am honored to share this, for I

have long admired you. In a world that too much belongs to the rich and powerful, you play no favorites. All, rich or poor, will be taken into your cart sooner or later."

Now, Death was very pleased to hear him speak so. "I will give you any gift you wish for as a reward," she said.

"I have only one wish," the good-hearted man said, "that I might help those who are sick and suffering."

"Very well," said Death, "I will make you a *curandero*, a healer. All you must do is lay your hand on a sick person's brow, and he or she will be made well again. But you must *never* use your gift if you see me standing at the head of a sick person's bed. I will be there because God has decided to call the suffering one out of life. *No one* must keep me from gathering that soul into my cart."

The woodcutter readily agreed to this. With a quick nod of her head, Death sealed their bargain. Then she drove her cart away to the east, where the morning sun had begun to lighten the sky behind the mountains.

As José returned home, he wondered if he had had a waking dream. Surely, he told himself, he had not met *Manita Muerte* in fact.

Now it chanced that, on his way, he met old Luis, a friend of his. Luis was limping, because a burro had kicked him in the leg.

"Let me help you," José offered.

He started to put his arm around his friend's shoulder; but at his touch, Luis cried wonderingly, "My leg! You have healed my leg! How have you done this?"

Then José told the old man the story of his meeting with Death.

Astounded, Luis insisted on telling everyone they met about José's great gift. Soon young and old were coming to him, asking for his blessing and begging for his healing touch.

The new *curandero* used his powers carefully. Quite by accident, since his only goal was to help the sick and pain-ridden, the healer himself grew wealthy. Still, he remained a generous person, and gave away as much gold as he kept.

Then one day José fell in love with Dolores, the daughter of old Luis. They longed to spend every moment in each other's company. Often Dolores would accompany him on his healing visits. There she would comfort an anxious husband or wife, or take a tearful child onto her lap, while José prayed over the ailing person and worked his wonderful cures through the gentle touch of his hands.

On the day before they were to be married, Dolores fell ill. When he was summoned to her bedside by her grieving father, José was distressed to see that Death was leaning upon one post at the head of the bed.

For the first and only time, José disobeyed *Manita Muerte*. He gently laid his hand upon Dolores's fevered brow and healed the young woman. At that instant, Death vanished from the room.

But as the *curandero* walked home late that night, Death's cart appeared on the road in front of him. When he dared look into the face of Death, he saw only a shadow underneath her cowl. He began to tremble.

Suddenly the moon and stars vanished. There was a moment of blinding darkness, and then he found himself in a cave filled with uncounted numbers of flickering candles. Death sat in her cart beside him. Slowly she raised a bony finger and pointed to a long and a short candle side by side on a nearby flat stone. The short candle had almost burned out.

"I warned you never to cure someone if I stood at

the head of the bed, but you disobeyed me," Death said angrily. "Now you must suffer the consequences. Once you were the tall candle with a long life ahead, and the nearly extinguished one was your beloved. Your disobedience has reversed the two. Now *your* life candle is the short one."

"Have pity!" said the man, dropping to his knees and pleading with Death. "I did what I did because I couldn't live without Dolores, nor she without me."

"Then I will grant you one last mercy," said *Manita Muerte*. So saying, Sister Death leaned over and snuffed out both candles together.

In an instant, the dead man's soul was in the cart as it creaked and crept along the dusty road that leads to a distant, shadowed country. Beside him, in the silence, rode the soul of his beloved, as Death carried them out of the land of the living.

# READING FOR UNDERSTANDING

**1.** How did José react when he first met Sister Death? Was he afraid of her?

**2.** How did Sister Death show that she was pleased with him?

**3.** What agreement did he make with Sister Death? What was the one important condition?

**4.** How did José's life change when everyone found out about his gift? What didn't change?

**5.** What type of person was Dolores? Give evidence from the story for your answer.

**6.** What did the long and short candles represent? What happened to them?

**7.** Why can no one keep Sister Death from gathering a soul into her cart?

# RESPONDING TO THE STORY

Imagine that you are in a situation similar to José's. Would you accept Sister Death's gift of healing powers? Would you obey her, or would you save the one you love, even if it meant that you could lose your own life? Write a paragraph that explains your answer.

# REVIEWING VOCABULARY

The sentences below are based on the story. Decide which of the words following the sentences best fits each blank. Write your answers on a separate sheet of paper.

**1.** When Sister Death told José never to use his gift if he saw her at a person's bed, he _____ agreed.

**2.** Luis was _____ when he heard José's story of his bargain with Sister Death.

**3.** José used his powers to help all those who were

_____.

**4.** José was _____ to Dolores's bedside.

**5.** José disobeyed Sister Death, and when she appeared before him, he saw only a shadow underneath her _____.

**6.** She angrily told José that he had to suffer the _____, and then she _____ both candles.

**Words:** _ailing, astounded, consequences, cowl, extinguished, readily, summoned_

## THINKING CRITICALLY

**1.** José said that he admired Sister Death. What were his reasons? Do you think that he still admired her at the end of the story? Why or why not?

**2.** José told Sister Death that he wanted to "help those who are sick and suffering." Judging from this request, what kind of person do you think he was?

**3.** How would you describe the character of Sister Death? Is she interesting? nasty? dull? unfair? Use details and examples from the story to support your response.

# Unit 5
## MAKING CHOICES

# A HORSEMAN IN THE SKY

## adapted from a story by Ambrose Bierce

From 1861 to 1865, the United States was torn apart by the Civil War. It was a war between the North and the South. Among the many disagreements between the two sides was the issue of slavery. The North wanted slavery made illegal in the United States. The South wanted to keep slaves working on the plantations.

In Southern states like Virginia, the Civil War tore families apart. Some family members supported the Southern cause, while others decided that the North was more just. Members of the same family ended up fighting on opposite sides.

The story you are about to read takes place in the South at the beginning of the Civil War. Father and son are torn apart when the son, Carter Druse, decides to fight for the North. As a result, Druse finds himself in a difficult situation. Just how difficult is something he never could have imagined. By the end of the story, he will have to make an almost impossible decision.

As you read "A Horseman in the Sky," think about what kind of man Carter Druse is. What might you do if you were in his situation? How do you feel about the final, shocking result of his action?

## VOCABULARY WORDS

**laurel** (LOHR-uhl) shrub with large, sweet-smelling leaves and greenish-yellow flowers
❖ The woman planted *laurel* throughout the backyard.

**detected** (dih-TEHK-tuhd) discovered
❖ They never *detected* who stole the painting.

**penalty** (PEHN-uhl-tee) punishment
❖ After he was found guilty, we waited to hear what his *penalty* would be.

**configuration** (kuhn-fihg-yuh-RAY-shuhn) an arrangement of parts; outline
❖ In the fog, we could see only the *configuration* of a person.

**concealed** (kuhn-SEELD) hid, kept secret
❖ The spy *concealed* his identity from the soldiers.

**sentinel** (SEHN-tih-nuhl) person who is stationed to keep watch
❖ The *sentinel* stood watching for signs of the enemy.

**betrayer** (bee-TRAY-ur) one who helps or supports the enemy or other side
❖ A *betrayer* is not loyal to troops or country.

**dispelled** (dihs-PEHLD) made to disappear
❖ My fears were *dispelled* when she called to say she was late.

**foe** (FOH) enemy
❖ His friend turned into his *foe* when he insulted him.

## KEY WORD

**Federal** (FED-uhr-uhl) Union
❖ He was a *Federal* officer, loyal to the North in the Civil War.

**O**ne sunny afternoon in the autumn of 1861, a soldier lay in a clump of evergreen bushes next to a road in western Virginia. He lay full length upon his stomach. His feet rested upon his toes, his head upon his left forearm. His extended right hand loosely grasped his rifle. Except for the movement of his limbs he seemed dead. He was asleep while on guard duty. If detected, he would have been shot dead, as the just and legal penalty for his crime.

The clump of laurel in which he lay was on a large flat rock, jutting out northward, overlooking a deep valley. The rock capped a high cliff. A stone dropped from its outer edge would have fallen straight down one thousand feet to the tops of the pines. Had he been awake, he would have had a view below that would have made him dizzy.

The country was wooded everywhere except at the bottom of the valley to the north. There, a small meadow, through which flowed a stream, was scarcely visible from the valley's rim. This open ground looked hardly larger than an ordinary dooryard. But it was really several acres in size. Its green was more vivid than that of the enclosing forest. Beyond it, rose a line of giant cliffs. The configuration of the valley, indeed, was such that, from where he was, it seemed entirely shut in. One wondered how the road could have found a way into and out of the valley

However, no place is too wild and difficult for men not to wage war in it. Concealed in the forest at the bottom of that military rat-trap were five regiments of Federal infantry. They had marched all the previous day and night, and were resting. At nightfall, they would take to the road again. They planned to climb to

**157**

where their unfaithful sentinel now slept, in order to descend the other slope and attack a camp of the enemy at about midnight.

The sleeping sentinel in the clump of laurel was a young Virginian named Carter Druse. He was the only child of wealthy parents. He had led a privileged life in the mountain country of western Virginia. His home was but a few miles from where he now lay. One morning, he had gotten up from the breakfast table and said, quietly but gravely: "Father, a Union regiment has arrived at Grafton. I am going to join it."

The father lifted his head. He looked at the son a moment in silence, and replied: "Well, go, sir, and whatever may occur, do what you conceive to be your duty. Virginia, to which you are a betrayer, must get on without you. Should we both live to the end of the war, we will speak further of the matter. Your mother, as the physician informed you, is in a most critical condition. At best she cannot be with us longer than a few weeks. But that time is precious. It would be better not to disturb her."

Carter Druse bowed respectfully to his father, who returned the salute with a stately courtesy that covered up a breaking heart. Druse then left the home of his childhood to become a soldier. By acts of courage and by deeds of devotion and daring, he soon earned the respect of his fellow soldiers and his officers. Because of his good record and his knowledge of his country he was chosen for his present dangerous duty as a sentry. Nevertheless, fatigue overcame his devotion to duty, and he had fallen asleep. What good or bad angel came in a dream to awaken him, who shall say? He quietly raised his forehead from his arm and looked through stems of the laurels. Instinctively, he closed his right hand around the stock of his rifle.

He then saw something that looked like a painting. At the edge of the huge cliff—motionless and sharply outlined against the sky—was a rider on horseback looking like a majestic statue. It was a man in gray uniform, sitting straight and soldierly on his horse. A rifle lay across the high, front part of the saddle, kept in place by the right hand grasping it at the "grip." The left hand, holding the thin leather straps, was invisible. The dark profile of the horse against the sky seemed sharply cut. The face of the rider, turned slightly away, showed only an outline of temple and beard. He was looking downward to the bottom of the valley. Magnified against the sky and by Druse's fear of a nearby enemy, the man on the horse appeared to be of enormous size.

For an instant, Druse had a strange feeling that he had slept to the end of the war. He imagined that he was looking upon a noble work of art—built upon that beautiful sky—to keep alive the heroic acts of which he had been but a small part. The feeling was dispelled by a slight movement of the horse. Without moving its feet, it had drawn its body slightly backward from the edge of the cliff. The man remained motionless as before. Fully awake and keenly aware of the significance of the situation, Druse now brought the butt of his rifle against his cheek. He pushed the barrel forward through the bushes and cocked the piece. Glancing through the sights, he aimed his rifle at a vital spot of the horseman's chest. A touch upon the trigger, and it would have been all over. At that instant, however, the horseman turned his head and looked in the direction of his concealed foe. He seemed to look into his very face, into his eyes, and into his brave, compassionate heart.

Carter Druse grew pale. All of his limbs shook, and he felt faint. His hand fell away from his weapon. His head slowly dropped until his face rested on the pile of leaves in which he lay. This courageous gentleman and strong soldier was close to fainting from intensity of emotion.

It was not for long. In another moment, he raised his head from the earth. His hands took their places on the rifle. His forefinger sought the trigger. Mind, heart, and eyes were clear. Conscience and reason were sound. He could not hope to capture that enemy. To alarm him would only send him dashing to his camp. Druse's duty was plain: the man must be shot dead from ambush—without warning, without a moment's spiritual preparation, without even an unspoken prayer. But—there is a hope. Maybe the rider is just admiring the magnificence of the view. If permitted, he may turn and ride carelessly away in the direction from which he came. Surely, when he leaves, it will be possible to judge whether he knows the Northern troops are in the area. Druse now saw a wavy line of men and horses creeping across the green meadow. Some foolish commander was permitting his soldiers to water their beasts in the open, in plain view from a dozen surrounding summits!

Druse withdrew his eyes from the valley and fixed them again upon the man and horse in the sky, and again it was through the sights of his rifle. But this time, his aim was at the horse. In his memory rang the words of his father at their parting: "Whatever may occur, do what you conceive to be your duty." He was calm now. His teeth were firmly but not rigidly closed. His nerves were as calm as a sleeping babe's. Not a tremor affected any muscle of his body. His breathing, until suspended in the act of taking aim, was regular and slow. Duty had conquered—the spirit had said to the body: "Peace, be still." He fired.

An officer of the Federal force had made his way to the lower edge of a small open space near the foot of the cliff. A quarter-mile before him, the gigantic face of rock rose from its nearby pines, towering so high above him that it made him dizzy to look up to where its edge cut a sharp, uneven line against the sky. Lifting his eyes to the dizzy height of its topmost point, the officer saw an astonishing sight—a man on horseback riding down into the valley through the air!

Straight upright sat the rider, in military fashion, with a firm seat in the saddle, a strong clutch on the rein to hold his charger from too forceful a plunge. His long hair streamed upward from his bare head, waving like a plume. His hands were concealed in the cloud of the horse's lifted mane. The animal's body was as straight as if every hoof-stroke encountered the resistant earth. Its motions were those of a wild gallop. Just as the officer looked, the horse moved sharply forward as in the act of settling down from a leap. But this was a flight!

Filled with amazement and terror by this ghost-like figure of a horseman in the sky, the officer was overcome by the intensity of his emotions. His legs failed him, and he fell. Almost at the same instant, he heard a crashing sound in the trees—a sound that died without an echo—and all was still.

The officer rose to his feet, trembling. The familiar sensation of a scraped knee reminded him of what had happened. He returned to camp a half-hour later.

This officer was a wise man. He knew better than to tell an incredible truth. He said nothing of what he had seen.

After firing his shot, Private Carter Druse reloaded his rifle and resumed his watch. Ten minutes had hardly passed when a Federal sergeant crept cautiously to him on hands and knees. Druse neither turned his head nor looked at him, but lay without motion or sign of recognition.

"Did you fire?" the sergeant whispered.

"Yes."

"At what?"

"A horse. It was standing on yonder rock—pretty far out. You see it is no longer there. The horse went over the cliff."

Druse's face was white, but he showed no other sign of emotion. Having answered, he turned away his eyes and said no more. The sergeant did not understand Druse's reaction.

"See here, Druse," he said, after a moment's silence,

"it's no use making a mystery. I order you to report.
Was there anybody on the horse?"

"Yes."

"Well, who was it?"

"My father."

The sergeant rose to his feet and walked away.
"Good God!" he said.

# READING FOR UNDERSTANDING

**1.** At the beginning of the story, Druse was **(a)** sleeping at his post **(b)** trying hard to stay awake **(c)** about to be killed.

**2.** Druse was a **(a)** poor man from the North **(b)** wealthy man from the South who joins the Union Army **(c)** wealthy man who was loyal to Virginia.

**3.** If Druse's mother had known that he had joined the Union Army, she would probably have **(a)** gotten better **(b)** told her husband to join him **(c)** died even sooner.

**4.** Carter's father **(a)** meant everything he said **(b)** was hiding his true feelings **(c)** knew his son would change his mind.

**5.** When the horseman looked in his direction, Druse **(a)** didn't know if it was the enemy **(b)** shot him quickly **(c)** felt many different feelings.

**6.** The saying that best fits this story is **(a)** Duty conquers all **(b)** Blood is thicker than water **(c)** Honor thy father.

# RESPONDING TO THE STORY

Think about a conflict between responsibility and feelings for family members or friends. For example, imagine that you are a police officer and you see a friend breaking the law. Which is more important for you to consider—your job and the law, or your friendship? Why?

## REVIEWING VOCABULARY

The sentences below are based on the story. Decide which of the words following the sentences best fits each blank. Write your answers on a separate sheet of paper.

1. Five regiments were _____ in the forest.
2. Carter Druse was a sleeping _____ in a clump of _____.
3. Death was the _____ for sleeping at your post.
4. If _____ sleeping, Carter would be shot.
5. The _____ of the valley made it hard to enter or leave.
6. At first, the horseman seemed like a statue, but this idea was _____ when the horse moved.
7. The horseman turned his head and looked directly at his _____.

**Words:** *laurel, configuration, detected, dispelled, penalty, concealed, sentinel, foe*

## THINKING CRITICALLY

1. Druse felt a conflict of emotions when he joined the Union army. It could not have been easy for him to make that choice. What kind of man do you think he was?
2. Druse's father told him to do what he thought he had to do. Which do you think is more important: duty to one's country or duty to one's family? Explain your choice.

**165**

# AFTER TWENTY YEARS

## adapted from a story by O. Henry

*Have you ever been surprised? Surely you have. In fact, everyone gets at least one big surprise in life. That's why people like to read stories with surprises. This is such a story.*

*The two characters in the story each get a big surprise. But neither surprise is a happy one. Two men had planned to meet again after twenty years' time. They do meet, but not in the way they had thought they would.*

*O. Henry is a writer who is famous for his surprise endings. Readers love them. Perhaps O. Henry was so good at writing surprise endings because his own life was full of surprises. For example, he was an editor and a prisoner at the same time. He began writing short stories while he was in jail. He became a very popular and successful writer. As you read this story, see if you can predict its surprise ending.*

# VOCABULARY WORDS

**guardian** (GAHR-dee-uhn) protector
* ❖ The *guardian* of a treasure has to defend it.

**reassuringly** (ree-uh-SHOOR-ihng-lee) in a convincing way
* ❖ Because he spoke so *reassuringly*, we never thought he was wanted by the police.

**plodder** (PLAHD-duhr) person who moves slowly and without imagination
* ❖ A *plodder* will always need an extra share of good luck to get ahead in life.

**moderately** (MAHD-uhr-iht-lee) somewhat, to some extent
* ❖ That movie was not a hit, but it did *moderately* well at the box office.

**submerged** (sub-MUHRJD) buried, hidden
* ❖ Because the logs were *submerged* in the pond, we could not see them.

# KEY WORDS

**scarfpin** (SKAHRF-pihn) pin similar to a tie clasp
* ❖ The *scarfpin* he wore held a diamond.

**wires** (WEYERZ) sends a message by telegraph
* ❖ When one police department *wires* another, the message is often about a wanted criminal.

**The policeman on the beat** moved up the avenue impressively. The way he walked was from habit, and not for show, because spectators were few. The time was barely 10 o'clock at night, but chilly gusts of wind with a taste of rain in them had nearly emptied the streets.

Trying doors as he went, twirling his club with many intricate and artful movements, turning now and then to cast his watchful eye down the quiet street, the officer made a fine picture of a guardian of the peace. The area was one that kept early hours. Now and then you might see the lights of a cigar store or of an all-night lunch counter, but the majority of the business places had long since closed for the night.

About midway down a certain block, the policeman suddenly slowed his walk. In the doorway of a darkened hardware store, a man leaned, with an unlighted cigar in his mouth. As the policeman walked up to him, the man spoke up quickly.

"It's all right, officer," he said reassuringly. "I'm just waiting for a friend. It's an appointment made twenty years ago. Sounds a little funny to you, doesn't it? Well, I'll explain if you'd like to make certain it's all right. About that long ago there used to be a restaurant where this store stands—'Big Joe' Brady's restaurant."

"Until five years ago," said the policeman. "It was torn down then."

The man in the doorway struck a match and lit his cigar. The light showed a pale, square-jawed face with keen eyes, and a little white scar near his right eyebrow. His scarfpin was a large diamond, oddly set.

"Twenty years ago tonight," said the man. "I dined here at 'Big Joe' Brady's with Jimmy Wells, my best

**168**

friend and the finest chap in the world. He and I were
raised here in New York, just like two brothers, together. I was eighteen, and Jimmy was twenty. The next
morning, I was to start for the West to make my fortune. You couldn't have dragged Jimmy out of New
York—he thought it was the only place on earth. Well,
we agreed that night that we would meet again in this
spot exactly twenty years from that date and time, no
matter what our conditions might be or from what
distance we might have to come. We figured that in
twenty years each of us ought to have his destiny
worked out and his fortune made, whatever they were
going to be."

"It sounds pretty interesting," said the policeman.
"Rather a long time between meetings, though, it

seems to me. Haven't you heard from your friend since you left?"

"Well, yes, we corresponded for a time," said the other. "But after a year or two, we lost track of each other. You see, the West is a pretty big place, and I kept hustling around it pretty lively. But I know Jimmy will meet me here if he's alive, for he always was the truest, most loyal chap in the world. He'll never forget. I came a thousand miles to stand in this doorway tonight, and it's worth it if my old partner turns up."

The waiting man pulled out a handsome pocket-watch, its lid set with small diamonds.

"It's three minutes to ten," he announced. "It was at exactly ten o'clock when we parted here at the restaurant door."

"Did pretty well out West, did you?" asked the policeman.

"You bet! I hope Jimmy has done half as well. He was a kind of plodder, though, good fellow as he was. I've had to compete with some of the sharpest wits going to get my pile. A man gets in a groove in New York. It takes the West to put a razor-edge on him."

The policeman twirled his club and took a step or two away.

"I'll be on my way. Hope your friend comes around all right. Going to call time on him sharp?"

"I should say not!" said the other. "I'll give him half an hour at least. If Jimmy is alive on earth, he'll be here by that time. So long, officer."

"Good night, sir," said the policeman, passing on along his beat, trying doors as he went.

There was now a fine, cold drizzle falling, and the wind had risen from its uncertain puffs into a steady blow. The few people moving about in that quarter hurried dismally and silently along with coat collars

**170**

turned high and pocketed hands. And in the door of the hardware store, the man who had come a thousand miles to keep an uncertain appointment with the friend of his youth, smoked his cigar and waited.

After he waited about twenty minutes more, a tall man in a long overcoat, with the collar turned up to his ears, hurried across from the opposite side of the street. He went directly to the waiting man.

"Is that you, Bob?" he asked doubtfully.

"Is that you, Jimmy Wells?" cried the man waiting in the door.

"Bless my heart!" exclaimed the new arrival, grasping both the other's hands with his own. "It's Bob, sure as fate. I was certain I'd find you here if you were still in existence. Well, well, well! Twenty years is a long time. The old restaurant's gone, Bob, but I wish it had lasted, so we could have had another dinner there. How has the West treated you, old man?"

"It has given me everything I asked it for. You've changed lots, Jimmy. I never thought you were so tall by two or three inches."

"Oh, I grew a bit after I was twenty."

"Doing well in New York, Jimmy?"

"Moderately. I have a position in one of the city departments. Come on, Bob. We'll go around to a place I know and have a good long talk about old times."

The two men started up the street, arm in arm. The man from the West, his confidence enlarged by success, was beginning to outline the history of his career. The other, submerged in his overcoat, listened to the story with interest.

At the corner stood a drug store, brilliant with electric lights. When they came into the glare of the lights, each of them turned simultaneously to gaze upon the other's face.

The man from the West stopped suddenly and released his arm.

"You're not Jimmy Wells," he snapped. "Twenty years is a long time, but not long enough to change a man's nose from a Roman to a pug."

"It sometimes changes a good man into a bad one," said the tall man. "You've been under arrest for ten minutes, 'Silky' Bob. Chicago thinks you may have dropped over our way and wires us she wants to have a chat with you. Going quietly, are you? That's sensible. Now, before we go on to the station, here's a note I was asked to hand you. You may read it here at the window. It's from Patrolman Wells."

The man from the West unfolded the little piece of paper handed him. His hand was steady when he began to read, but it trembled a little by the time he had finished. The note was rather short.

> *Bob: I was at the appointed place on time. When you struck the match to light your cigar, I saw it was the face of the man wanted in Chicago. Somehow I couldn't do it myself, so I went around and got a plain-clothes man to do the job.*
>
> *"JIMMY."*

## READING FOR UNDERSTANDING

1. The story took place **(a)** in New York City **(b)** in the West **(c)** somewhere near Chicago.
2. Jimmy Wells was the best friend of **(a)** the policeman **(b)** Big Joe Brady **(c)** the man from the West.
3. Jimmy figured out who the man from the West really was when he **(a)** used his friend's old nickname **(b)** struck a match **(c)** pulled out his watch.
4. We can assume from the story that 'Silky' Bob made his money through **(a)** smart business deals **(b)** crime **(c)** saving.
5. The note from Jimmy shows that **(a)** he never cared for Bob **(b)** the old friendship still meant something to him **(c)** he was jealous of Bob.

## RESPONDING TO THE STORY

After twenty years, the two friends' lives have turned out very differently. Do you think that your life in twenty years' time might be very different from what you expect now? Write a paragraph explaining why or why not.

## REVIEWING VOCABULARY

The sentences below are based on the story. Decide which of the words following the sentences best fits each blank. Write your answers on a separate sheet of paper.

1. The man in the doorway did not want the policeman to suspect him, so he spoke to the officer _____.

2. The plainclothes man _____ himself in his overcoat so that Bob would not suspect that he was not Jimmy Wells.

**3.** Bob thought his friend Jimmy was kind of a
_____.

**4.** As a _____ of the peace, the officer patrolled his beat.

**5.** The man pretending to be Jimmy tells Bob that he has done _____ well in life.

**Words:** *plodder, submerged, guardian, moderately, reassuringly*

## THINKING CRITICALLY

**1.** After twenty years, Bob and Jimmy still think enough of each other to show up for this meeting. But when Jimmy recognizes Bob as a wanted man, he feels that he must do his duty as a law officer. Do you think Jimmy should have had Bob arrested, or should he have let Bob go free? Why?

**2.** Do you think that Bob respected Jimmy for doing his duty? Why or why not?

**3.** How does loyalty to a friend compare to the importance of duty to your job?

# THE OLD DEMON
## adapted from a story by Pearl S. Buck

*Old Mrs. Wang both loved and hated the river that flowed through her Chinese village. Its waters helped her crops to grow. But they could also overflow, causing great destruction. That is why Mrs. Wang sometimes called the unruly river "The Old Demon."*

*When the story you are about to read opens, China is being invaded by Japan. As the Japanese approach, all of the people in Mrs. Wang's village flee. Mrs. Wang sees the enemy coming, but she does not run away like the other villagers. Perhaps she is foolish to stay behind. But Mrs. Wang's curiosity gets the better of her. The planes that soar overhead and drop bombs look like great birds to her. The enemy that she encounters looks more like a familiar countryman than an enemy.*

*At the end of this story, even the Old Demon of a river has become Mrs. Wang's friend. Read the story to find out exactly how this twist happens.*

# VOCABULARY WORDS

**dike** (DYK) a dam built to prevent flooding by the sea or a river
❖ They needed to build the *dike* higher.

**tentatively** (TEHN-tuh-tihv-lee) hesitantly
❖ Though I needed more details, I *tentatively* agreed to go.

**discern** (dih-SERN) recognize clearly
❖ I could not *discern* the author's main idea.

**acutely** (uh-KYOOT-lee) sharply, keenly
❖ The stain on his necktie was *acutely* embarrassing.

**sluice** (SLOOS) an artificial channel or passage for water
❖ They'll need a *sluice* if they want to water that land.

**resolutely** (REHZ-uh-loot-lee) firmly
❖ The batter stepped *resolutely* up to the plate and swung.

**wrenched** (REHNCHD) twisted or pulled suddenly
❖ The broken door had to be *wrenched* off its hinges.

# KEY WORDS

**Yellow River** river in China, about 3,000 miles long
❖ Throughout history, the *Yellow River* has been famous in China for its serious floods.

**Buddhist** (BOOD-ist) a person who believes in the religion of Buddhism.
❖ She is a devout *Buddhist*.

**purgatory** (PER-guh-tawr-ee) in certain religious beliefs, a place in which the souls of dead persons suffer until they amend for their sins
❖ In Roman Catholic teachings, *purgatory* exists.

**176**

**O**ld **Mrs. Wang knew** of course that there was a war. Everybody had known for a long time that there was a war going on and that Japanese were killing Chinese. To Mrs. Wang, however, the war was not real and no more than rumor since none of the Wangs had been killed. Old Mrs. Wang's clan village, the Village of Three Mile Wangs, on the flat banks of the Yellow River, had never even seen a Japanese person. Only the war caused them to talk about the Japanese.

It was an early summer evening. After her supper, Mrs. Wang had climbed the dike steps, as she did daily, to see how high the river had risen. She was more afraid of the river than of the Japanese. She knew what the river could do. One by one, the villagers had followed her up the dike. They stood staring down at the mischievous yellow water, which was curling along like a lot of snakes and biting at the high dike banks.

"I never saw it as high as this so early," Mrs. Wang said. She sat down on a bamboo stool that her grandson, Little Pig, had brought for her, and spat into the water.

"It's worse than the Japanese, this old devil of a river," Little Pig said recklessly.

"Fool!" said Mrs. Wang quickly. "The river god will hear you. Talk about something else."

So they had gone on talking about the Japanese. How, for instance, asked Wang, the baker, would they know the Japanese when they saw them?

Mrs. Wang at this point said positively, "You'll know them. I once saw a foreigner. He was taller than the roof of my house, and he had mud-colored hair and eyes the color of a fish's eyes. Anyone who does not look like us—that is a Japanese."

Everyone listened to her since she was the oldest woman in the village.

Then Little Pig spoke up in his unsettling way. "You can't see them, Grandmother. They hide up in the sky in airplanes."

Mrs. Wang did not answer immediately. Once, she would have said positively, "I shall not believe in an airplane until I see it." But so many things had been true that she had not believed. So now, she merely stared quietly around the dike, where they all sat around her. The evening was very pleasant and cool, and she felt that nothing mattered so long as the river did not rise to flood.

"I don't believe in the Japanese," she said flatly.

They laughed at her a little, but no one spoke. Someone lit her pipe. It was Little Pig's wife, who was her favorite.

"Sing, Little Pig!" someone called.

So Little Pig began to sing an old song in a high, shaky voice, and old Mrs. Wang listened and forgot the Japanese. The evening was beautiful. And the sky was so clear and still that the willows overhanging the dike were reflected even in the muddy water. Everything was at peace. The thirty-odd houses which made up the village were spread out along beneath the willow trees. Nothing could break this peace. After all, the Japanese were only human beings.

"I doubt those airplanes," she said mildly to Little Pig when he stopped singing.

But without answering her, Little Pig went on to another song.

Year in and year out she had spent the summer evenings like this on the dike—ever since she had been seventeen and a bride. Her husband had shouted to her to come out of the house and up to the dike. She had

**178**

come, blushing and twisting her hands together to hide among the women, while the men roared at her and made jokes about her. All the same, they had liked her. "A pretty piece of meat in your bowl," they had said to her husband. "Her feet are a trifle big," he had answered, trying to make her seem less special. But she could see that he was pleased, and so, gradually, her shyness went away.

He, poor man, had been drowned in a flood when he was still young. And it had taken her years to get him prayed out of Buddhist purgatory. Finally, she had grown tired of it, for she had the responsibilities of caring for a child and maintaining the land. So when the priest said persuasively, "Another ten pieces of silver and he'll be out entirely," she asked, "What does he have in there yet?"

"Only his right hand," the priest said, encouraging her.

Well, then, her patience broke. Ten dollars! It would feed them for the winter. Besides, she had had to hire labor for her share of repairing the dike so there would be no more floods.

"If it's only one hand, he can pull himself out," she said firmly.

She often wondered if he had, poor silly fellow. Like it or not, she often had thought gloomily in the night that he was still lying there, waiting for her to do something about it. That was the sort of man he was. Well, some day, perhaps, when Little Pig's wife had had the first baby safely and she had a little extra money, she might go back to get him out of purgatory. There was no real hurry, though.

"Grandmother, you must go in," Little Pig's wife's soft voice said. "There is a mist rising from the river, now that the sun is gone."

"Yes, I suppose I must," old Mrs. Wang agreed. She gazed at the river a moment. That river—it was full of good and evil together. It would water the fields when it was restrained and checked. But if an inch were allowed it, it crashed through the dike like a roaring dragon. That was how her husband had been swept away. Careless, he was, about his bit of the dike. He was always going to mend it, always going to pile more earth on top of it, and then, one night, the river rose and broke through. He had run out of the house. She had climbed on the roof with her child and had saved the two of them while her husband drowned. Well, they had pushed the river back again behind its dikes, and it had stayed there this time. Every day, she herself walked up and down the length of the dike for which the village was responsible and examined it. The men laughed and said, "If anything is wrong with the dike, Granny will tell us."

It had never occurred to any of them to move the village away from the river. The Wangs had lived there for generations. Some had always escaped the floods and had fought the river more fiercely than ever afterward.

Little Pig suddenly stopped singing.

"The moon is coming up!" he cried. "That's not good. Airplanes come out on moonlit nights."

"Where did you learn all this about airplanes?" old Mrs. Wang asked. "It is tiresome to me," she added, so severely that no one spoke. In this silence, leaning upon the arm of Little Pig's wife, she slowly descended the earthen steps that led down into the village. She held the long pipe in her other hand as a walking stick. Behind her, the villagers came down, one by one, to bed. No one moved before she did, but none stayed long after her.

**180**

In her own bed at last, behind the blue cotton mosquito curtains that Little Pig's wife fastened securely, she soon fell peacefully asleep. But first, she lay awake a little while, thinking about the Japanese and wondering why they wanted to fight. Only very crude people wanted wars. In her mind, she saw large crude people. If they came, one must influence them, she thought. One must invite them to drink tea, and explain things to them, reasonably. Only why would they come to a peaceful farming village?

So, she was not in the least prepared for Little Pig's wife screaming at her that the Japanese had come. She sat up in bed muttering, "The tea bowls—the tea—"

"Grandmother, there's no time!" Little Pig's wife screamed. "They're here—they're here!"

"Where?" old Mrs. Wang cried, now awake.

"In the sky!" Little Pig's wife wailed.

They had all run out, into the clear early dawn, and gazed up. There, like wild geese flying in the autumn, were great birdlike shapes.

"But what are they?" old Mrs. Wang cried.

And then, like a silver egg dropping, something drifted straight down and fell at the far end of the village in a field. A fountain of earth flew up, and they all ran to see it. There was a hole thirty feet across, as big as a pond. They were so surprised that they could not speak. And then, before anybody could say anything, another egg and another began to fall. Everybody began running.

Everybody, that is, but Mrs. Wang. When Little Pig's wife seized her hand to drag her along, old Mrs. Wang pulled away and sat down against the bank of the dike.

"I can't run," she remarked. "I haven't run in seventy years, since before my feet were bound. You go on. Where's Little Pig?" She looked around. Little Pig was already gone. "Like his grandfather," she remarked, "always the first to run."

But Little Pig's wife would not leave Mrs. Wang—not, that is, until the old woman reminded her that it was her duty.

"If Little Pig is dead," she said, "then it is necessary that his son be born alive." And when the girl still hesitated, she struck at her gently with her pipe. "Go on—go on!" she exclaimed.

So unwillingly, because now they could scarcely hear each other speak above the roar of the dipping planes, Little Pig's wife went on with the others.

By now, although only a few minutes had passed, the village was in ruins; the straw roofs and wooden beams were blazing. Everybody was gone. As the villagers passed, they shrieked at old Mrs. Wang to come on, and she had called back pleasantly, "I'm coming, I'm coming!"

But she did not go. She sat quite alone, watching what was an extraordinary spectacle. For, soon, other planes came, from where she did not know, but they attacked the first ones. The sun came up over the fields of ripening wheat. And in the clear summery air, the planes wheeled and darted and spat at each other.

"I'd like to see one of them up close," she said aloud. And at that moment, as though in answer, one of them pointed suddenly downward. Wheeling and twisting as though it were wounded, it fell head down in a field which Little Pig had ploughed only yesterday for soybeans. And in an instant, the sky was empty again, and there was only this wounded thing on the ground and herself.

She hoisted herself up carefully from the earth. At her age she need be afraid of nothing. She had lived a good, long life. She could, she decided, go and see what it was. So, leaning on her bamboo pipe, she made her way slowly across the fields. Behind her in the sudden stillness, two or three village dogs appeared and followed, creeping close to her in their terror. When they drew near to the fallen plane, they barked furiously. Then she hit them with her pipe.

"Be quiet!" she scolded, "there's already been noise enough to split my ears!"

She tapped the airplane.

"Metal," she told the dogs. "Silver, doubtless," she added. Melted down, it would make them all rich.

She walked around it, examining it closely. What made it fly? It seemed dead. Nothing moved or made a sound within it. Then, coming to the side to which it was tipped, she saw a young man in it. He was in a heap in a little seat. The dogs growled, but she struck at them again, and they fell back.

"Are you dead?" she inquired politely.

The young man moved a little at her voice but did not speak. She drew nearer and peered into the hole in which he sat. His side was bleeding.

"Wounded!" she exclaimed. She took his wrist. It was warm, but still. When she let it go, it dropped against the side of the hole. She stared at him. He had black hair and dark skin like a Chinese person, and still he did not look like a Chinese.

"He must be a Southerner," she thought. Well, the chief thing was that he was alive.

"You had better come out," she remarked. "I'll put some herb plaster on your side."

The young man muttered something slowly.

"What did you say?" she asked the man. But he did not say it again.

"I am still quite strong," she decided for a moment. So she reached in and seized him around the waist and pulled him out slowly, panting a good deal. Fortunately, he was a rather little fellow and very light. When she had him on the ground, he seemed to find his feet. He stood shakily and clung to her, and she held him up.

"Now, if you can walk to my house," she said, "I'll see if it is still there."

Then he said something, quite clearly. She listened and could not understand a word of it. She pulled away from him and stared.

"What's that?" she asked.

He pointed at the dogs. They stood growling, the hair on their necks standing up. Then he spoke again, and as he spoke he crumpled to the ground. The dogs fell on him, so that she had to beat them off with her hands.

"Get away!" she shouted at the dogs. "Who told you to kill him?"

And then, when they had moved back quietly, she heaved him somehow onto her back. Trembling, half carrying, half pulling him, she dragged him to the ruined village and laid him in the street while she went to find her house, taking the dogs with her.

Her house was quite gone. She found the place easily enough. This was where it should be, opposite the water gate into the dike. She had always watched that gate herself. Miraculously, it was not damaged now, nor was the dike broken. It would be easy enough to rebuild the house. It was gone only for the present.

So she went back to the young man. He was lying as she had left him, propped against the dike, panting and very pale. He had opened his coat and had a little bag, from which he was taking out strips of cloth and a bottle of something. And again he spoke, and again she understood nothing. Then he made signs, and she saw it was water that he wanted, so she picked up one of many broken pots that had been blown around the street. Then, going up the dike, she filled it with water and brought it down again and washed his wound. She tore off the strips that he had made from the rolls of bandaging. He knew how to put the cloth over the gaping wound. He made signs to her, and she followed these signs. All the time he was trying to tell her something, but she could understand nothing.

"You must be from the South, sir," she said. It was easy to see that he had no education. He looked very clever. "I have heard that your language is different from ours." She laughed a little to put him at ease, but he only stared at her darkly and gloomily. So she said brightly, "Now if I could find something for us to eat, it would be nice."

He did not answer. Indeed, he lay back, panting still more heavily, and stared into space as though she had not spoken.

"You would feel better with food," she went on. "And so would I," she added. She was beginning to feel unbearably hungry.

It occurred to her that there might be some bread in the baker's shop. Even if it were dusty from fallen cannon shells, it would still be bread. She would go and see. But before she went, she moved the soldier a little so that he lay in the edge of a willow tree's shadow. Then she went to the baker's shop. The dogs were gone.

The baker's shop was, like everything else, in ruins. No one was there. At first, she saw nothing but the mass of crumpled earthen walls. But then she remembered that the oven was just inside the door. The door frame still stood erect, supporting one end of the roof. She stood in this frame, and, running her hand in underneath the fallen roof, she felt the wooden cover of the iron kettle. Under this, there might be steamed bread. She worked her arm in delicately and carefully. It took quite a long time, and clouds of lime and dust almost choked her. Nevertheless, she was right. She squeezed her hand in under the cover and felt the firm, smooth skin of the big steamed rolls. She drew out four, one by one.

"It's hard to kill an old thing like me," she remarked cheerfully to no one. She began to eat one of the rolls as she walked back. If she only had a bit of garlic and a bowl of tea—but one couldn't have everything in these times.

It was at this moment that she heard voices. When she came in sight of the soldier, she saw surrounding him a crowd of other soldiers, who had apparently come from nowhere. They were staring down at the wounded soldier, whose eyes were now closed.

"Where did you get this Japanese, Old Mother?" they shouted at her.

"What Japanese?" she said, coming to them.

"This one!" they shouted.

"Is he a Japanese?" she cried in the greatest astonishment. "But he looks like us. His eyes are black, his skin—"

"Japanese!" one of them shouted at her.

"Well," she said quietly, "he dropped out of the sky."

"Give me that bread!" another shouted.

"Take it," she said, "all except this one for him."

"A Japanese pilot eat good bread?" the soldier shouted at her.

"I suppose he is hungry also," old Mrs. Wang replied. She began to dislike these men. But then, she had always disliked soldiers.

"I wish you would go away," she said. "What are you doing here? Our village has always been peaceful."

"It certainly looks very peaceful now," one of the

**186**

men said, grinning, "as peaceful as a grave. Do you know who did that, Old Mother? The Japanese!"

"I suppose so," she agreed. Then she asked. "Why? That's what I don't understand."

"Why? Because they want our land, that's why!"

"Our land!" she repeated. "Why, they can't have our land!"

"Never!" they shouted.

But all this time, while they were talking and chewing the bread that they had divided among themselves, they were watching the eastern horizon.

"Why do you keep looking east?" old Mrs. Wang now asked.

"The Japanese are coming from there," the man who had taken the bread replied.

"Are you running away from them?" she asked, surprised.

"There are only a handful of us," he said apologetically.

"We were left to guard a village—Pao An—in the country of—"

"I know that village," old Mrs. Wang interrupted. "You needn't tell me. I was a girl there. How is the old Pao who keeps the tea shop in the main street? He's my brother."

"Everybody is dead there," the old man replied. "The Japanese have taken it. A great army of men came with their foreign guns and tanks. What could we do?"

"Of course, only run," she agreed. Nevertheless she felt dazed and sick. So, he was dead, her one remaining brother. She was now the last of her father's family.

The soldiers were scattering, again leaving her alone.

"They'll be coming, those Japanese soldiers," they were saying. "We'd best go on."

Nevertheless, the one who had taken the bread lingered a moment to stare down at the wounded man, who lay with his eyes shut, not having moved at all.

"Is he dead?" he inquired. Then, before Mrs. Wang could answer, he pulled a short knife out of his belt. "Dead or not, I'll give him a punch or two with this!"

But old Mrs. Wang pushed his arm away.

"No, you won't!" she said with authority. "If he is dead, then there is no use sending him to purgatory all in pieces. I am a good Buddhist myself."

The man laughed. "Oh, well, he is dead," he answered. Then, seeing his comrades already at a distance, he ran after them.

A Japanese, was he? Old Mrs. Wang, left alone with the wounded man, looked at him tentatively. He was very young, she could see, now that his eyes were closed. His hand, limp in his state of unawareness, looked like a boy's hand, unformed and still growing. She felt his wrist but could discern no pulse. She leaned over him and held to his lips the half of her roll which she had not eaten.

"Eat!" she said very loudly and distinctly. "Bread!"

But there was no answer. Evidently he was dead. He must have died while she had been getting the bread out of the oven.

There was nothing to do but to finish the bread herself. When that was done, she wondered if she should follow after Little Pig and his wife and all the villagers. The sun was mounting and it was growing hot. If she were going to follow them, she had better go now.

But first, she would climb the dike and see what the direction was. They had gone straight west, and as far as the eye could see westward was a great plain.

So she climbed the dike slowly, getting very hot. There was a slight breeze on top of the dike, and it felt good. She was shocked to see the river very near the top of the dike. Why, it had risen in the last hour!

"You old demon!" she said severely. Let the river god hear it if he liked. He was evil, that he was, to threaten a flood when there had been all this other trouble.

Just as she was about to climb down, she saw something on the eastern horizon. It looked at first like an immense cloud of dust. But, as she stared at it, it very quickly became a lot of black dots and shining spots. Then she saw what it was. It was a lot of men—an army! Instantly, she knew what army.

"That's the Japanese!" she thought. Yes, above them were the buzzing silver planes. They circled about, seeming to search for someone.

"I don't know who you're looking for," she muttered,

"unless it's me and Little Pig and his wife. We're the only ones left. You've already killed my brother Pao."

She had almost forgotten that Pao was dead. Now she remembered it acutely. He had such a nice shop—always clean, and the tea good and the best meat dumplings to be had and the price always the same. Pao was a good man. Besides, what about his wife and his seven children? Doubtless, they had all been killed, too. Now, these Japanese were looking for her. It occurred to her that she could easily be seen on the dike. So she clambered hastily down.

It was when she was about halfway down that she thought of the water gate. This old river—it had been a curse to them since time began. Why should it not make up a little now for all the wickedness that it had done? It was plotting wickedness again, trying to steal over its banks. Well, why not? For a moment, she could not decide. It was a pity, of course, that the young dead Japanese would be swept away by the flood. He was a nice-looking boy, and she had saved him from being stabbed. It was not quite the same as saving his life, of course, but it was still a little the same. If he had been alive, he would have been saved. She went over to him and tugged at him until he lay near the top of the bank. Then she came down again.

She knew perfectly well how to open the water gate. Any child knew how to open the sluice for crops. But she also knew how to swing open the whole gate. The question was, could she open it quickly enough to get out of the way?

"I'm only one old woman," she muttered. She hesitated a second more. It would be a pity not to see what sort of a baby that Little Pig's wife would have, but one could not see everything. She had seen a great deal in this life. There was an end to what one could see.

She glanced again to the east. There were the Japanese, coming across the plain. They were a long clear line of black, dotted with thousands of glittering points. If she opened this gate, the rushing water would roar toward them, rushing into the plains, rolling into a wide lake, maybe drowning them. Certainly, they could not keep on marching nearer and nearer to her and to Little Pig and his wife as they waited for her. Well, Little Pig and his wife—they would wonder about her—but they would never dream of this. It would make a good story. She would have enjoyed telling it.

She turned resolutely to the gate. Some people fight with airplanes and with guns, but you could fight with a river, too, if it were a wicked one like this one. She wrenched out a huge wooden pin. It was slippery with silvery green moss. The trickle of water burst into a strong jet. When she wrenched one more pin, the rest would give way. She began pulling at it and felt it slip a little from its hole.

"I might be able to get myself out of purgatory with this," she thought, "and maybe they'll let me have that old man of mine, too. What's a hand of his compared to all this? Then we'll—"

The pin slipped away, and the gate burst flat against her and knocked her breath away. She had only time to gasp to the river: "Come on, you old demon!"

Then she felt it seize her and lift her up to the sky. It was beneath her and around her. It rolled her joyfully here and there. Then, holding her close and embracing her, it went rushing against the enemy.

# READING FOR UNDERSTANDING

**1.** Arrange the following incidents in the order in which they occurred:

(a) A Japanese plane crashed in a field.

(b) Mrs. Wang tried to save the wounded pilot.

(c) The Japanese airplanes soared over Mrs. Wang's village.

(d) Mrs. Wang released the flood gate. The river lifted her up and rushed forth to the enemy.

(e) Mrs. Wang learned that the Japanese had killed everyone in her old village, Pao An.

**2.** Why did all the villagers except for Mrs. Wang run away?

**3.** Why do you think Mrs. Wang didn't treat the young pilot as an enemy, especially after she found out that he was Japanese?

**4.** Why did Mrs. Wang open the water gate, knowing that this action would almost certainly lead to her death?

**5.** Who do you think "the old demon" is in the story?

# RESPONDING TO THE STORY

How did Mrs. Wang's actions summarize how she felt about war and the enemy? Use evidence from the story to support your view.

## REVIEWING VOCABULARY

Match each word on the left with the correct definition on the right.

**1.** dike            **a.** twisted suddenly
**2.** tentatively     **b.** to recognize clearly
**3.** sluice         **c.** sharply
**4.** discern       **d.** a dam built to prevent
**5.** acutely               flooding
**6.** wrenched     **e.** artificial channel for water
**7.** resolutely     **f.** hesitantly
                        **g.** firmly

## THINKING CRITICALLY

**1.** How did the villagers regard old Mrs. Wang? Give examples from the story to support your view.
**2.** Mrs. Wang came from a tiny village. She had never seen an airplane, or a person from another country. Nevertheless, she struck a mighty blow against the enemy. Was Mrs. Wang wise or foolish? Write your opinion as a one-paragraph essay.
**3.** Mrs. Wang's grandson, Little Pig, left the village without her. How do you think he felt when he realized she had not followed? What do you think he would have said if he had found out how she had stopped the Japanese?

# A SOLDIER'S TALE

## Carroll Moulton

*The Revolutionary War began in 1775 and ended in 1783. The American colonies fought this war to gain independence from Britain.*

*Led by General George Washington, the colonists fought bravely against the better-equipped British. The troops also battled freezing weather, food shortages, and Tories. Tories were colonists who were loyal to Britain. They did what they could to help the British win the war.*

*"A Soldier's Tale" is taken from a diary written after the war. It was written by a brave soldier who made an amazing choice—and tried to keep it a secret. As you read, try to figure out this soldier's secret.*

# VOCABULARY WORDS

**commission** (kuh-MIHSH-uhn) a document that approves a soldier's military appointment
❖ When the cadets graduate, they will receive their *commissions*.

**torment** (TAWR-mehnt) great pain or anguish
❖ The doctors felt that surgery would end his *torment*.

**hoard** (HAWRD) secret supply
❖ Gretchen showed me her *hoard* of rare stamps.

**skirmish** (SKER-mihsh) brief fight
❖ After the *skirmish*, the troops fled into the woods.

**curtly** (KERT-lee) abruptly
❖ "Be quick!" the counselor yelled *curtly*.

**orderly** (AWR-duhr-lee) assistant to a military officer
❖ The general assigned all office duties to his *orderly*.

**mutiny** (MYOO-tuh-nee) rebellion against military superiors
❖ The sailors joined in a *mutiny* against the captain.

# KEY WORDS

**West Point** a town on the Hudson River in New York; the site of the U.S. Military Academy since 1802.
❖ During the Revolution, *West Point* was a fort and military reservation.

**Tories** (TAWR-eez) colonists who sided with the British during the American Revolution
❖ The soldiers called the *Tories* traitors.

*West Point    25 October 1783*

**I**t seems like such a long time ago that I joined the army. Actually, it has been only a year and a half since I received my commission as a soldier. The war has been officially over for nearly two months. During the war, I did not keep a diary, for fear it might somehow fall into the wrong hands. But now my secret is out . . .

I was born twenty-three years ago in Plympton, Massachusetts. My father loved adventure, and he left our family to sail the seas when I was a baby. Mother couldn't afford to bring up five children, so I spent my childhood in a series of foster homes.

There was my mother's cousin in Plympton, Miss Fuller, who took care of me and taught me to read. There was Mrs. Thatcher in Middleborough, who was so old that I had to take care of her, feeding her every meal! Then there was Deacon Thomas. I worked for the Thomases as an indentured servant. As such, I had to sign a contract agreeing to work for the Thomases for ten years. They made me chop wood, kill chickens, and tend the horses. By the time I was fourteen, I could take care of myself and anyone who needed help. I found that I liked difficult situations. I was filled with daring and longed for adventure.

Is that why I sneaked myself into the army? I was only fifteen when war broke out in April 1775. Full of envy, I watched the deacon's eldest son march off to join the army and fight the British. I told myself that my time would come.

After my contract with the deacon was up, I taught school for a while in Middleborough, but inside I was restless and unhappy. I kept asking myself why someone like me couldn't become a soldier in the army. So,

**196**

in May of 1782, I did just that. I walked the thirty-five miles to Boston and signed up.

My first two months in the army were a torment. The other soldiers teased me, saying I looked like a sissy. Instead of calling me Bobby, they embarrassed me with nicknames like Molly and Blooming Boy. What could I do? I was twenty-two, but they said I looked fifteen! On the first long march from Boston to West Point, I kept to myself. I knew the day would come when I'd show them that Private Robert Shurtliff deserved their respect!

Slowly, they began to like me. And slowly I began to learn that war was a less romantic adventure than I'd thought. Most of our duty was on anti-Tory scouting missions. During peacetime, the Tories were British sympathizers. Now they were traitors, and we hated them. While we often went hungry, they spied on us and stole and hid stores of food to give to the British.

It was on one of these scouting missions that my secret nearly came out. It was during the winter. The salt pork and bread were gone. It seemed the whole army was going hungry.

That day, about thirty of us had marched from White Plains across to Eastchester, north of New York City, looking for signs of Tory activity. Two boys led us to a cave. There were so many packages of food inside that we could scarcely believe the sight: cheese, honey, butter, bacon! We knew that stopping to eat would be dangerous because the Tories would come back to claim their hoard. But we ate anyway. Then we hid in the woods nearby, ready to spring a trap on them when they returned.

They came back after dark. There were about forty of them, and they were all on horseback. Still, we took them by surprise. There was a heated skirmish before they retreated. One of their officers managed to slash me across the forehead with a saber. My real problem, though, was the musket ball that hit my left thigh just as they disappeared into the woods.

Our sergeant helped me to a small village, where there was a hospital at the French army camp. There was so much blood from both wounds that I looked like a piece of meat straight from the butcher's. A young French surgeon bandaged my head. I hoped that he wouldn't notice my leg wound, but the blood seeping from my boot gave me away.

The surgeon began to tear my pant leg away from the wound, saying he would fix me up shortly. He yanked at the cloth so suddenly and strongly that it tore nearly to the top of my thigh.

"Mind your haste, and watch my leg!" I snapped at him curtly.

He had to dig deep to get the bullet out, and the pain was unbearable. But what he'd done to my trousers concerned me more.

Next, he wanted me to unbutton my shirt so he could listen to my heartbeat; he started to bend his head toward my chest.

"Listen to your own heartbeat!" I shouted angrily, and rudely pushed him away.

He was amazed by my unfriendly behavior and insisted on taking my pulse. I let him. But then I told him in no uncertain terms that I was fine now and just wanted to be left alone.

We had to go on another march two weeks after that. Every step was painful, and I began to think that my leg never would heal properly. A young soldier named Richard Snow marched next to me. Suddenly he lurched to the ground. He was ill with a high fever and could not continue.

I told the sergeant that I would take charge of him since the whole company could not afford to wait behind. I was able to get Snow to a farmhouse nearby. I tended to him regularly during his illness. A closeness developed between us, and he learned the secret I had never told anyone. We stayed ten days. Poor Richard Snow died from his fever, and the farmer's daughter helped me bury him.

General John Paterson chose me as his orderly at West Point in the beginning of spring. The days of sleeping on straw and going hungry were over. In June, the general sent me as part of an army detachment to put down a mutiny in Philadelphia. Some soldiers were demanding their back pay, but Congress had no money to give them. I also had never been paid a penny for my service, but I didn't want to see a war break out over this issue.

The mutiny had worn itself out by the time we reached Philadelphia. However, there was a beautiful city to see. I allowed myself to think that our long war might be ending at last, as I looked at the spot where the Declaration of Independence had been signed almost seven years before.

But fate still had another surprise for me in the City of Brotherly Love. At the camp one night, I suddenly felt faint. Then I started to shiver, just as Snow had. The shakes were uncontrollable, and I feared the worst. There had been an epidemic of fever among the soldiers for more than a week.

I must have lost consciousness, because my next memory is of an argument between two men. They were talking about who would get my clothes once I had been carried off to the new burying ground.

"I'm taking those boots," said one, "though they look rather small."

**199**

"Too bad to see such a downy-cheeked lad going to meet his Maker," said the other.

I realized that they considered me as good as dead. But even near death, my worst thought was that now someone would discover my secret.

I realized two things when I awoke from the fever. I was going to live, and my secret had been discovered. Now I am waiting for an appointment to see General Paterson.

I cannot say what the future now holds for me. All I know is that Dr. Barnabas Binney of Philadelphia, the physician who helped me, is the one who discovered my secret. I hold his letter to General Paterson in my hand. The letter informs General Paterson that his faithful orderly, Private Robert Shurtliff, is really Deborah Sampson of Plympton, Massachusetts.

## READING FOR UNDERSTANDING

**1.** Arrange the following incidents in the order in which they occurred:

   **(a)** The narrator took care of Richard Snow.

   **(b)** Dr. Binney discovered the narrator's true identity.

   **(c)** The narrator was badly wounded in the left thigh.

   **(d)** General Paterson sent the narrator to Philadelphia.

   **(e)** The narrator walked thirty-five miles to Boston and joined the army.

**2.** What kind of childhood do you think the narrator had? Use details from the story to explain your answer.

**3.** How did her experiences growing up prepare the narrator to be a soldier?

**4.** What taught Deborah Sampson that war was not a "romantic adventure"?

**5.** When was Deborah's identity almost revealed? What did she do to protect it?

**6.** List four or five adjectives that describe what Deborah Sampson was like. Use examples from the story to back up each word.

## RESPONDING TO THE STORY

This diary entry is based on real events in the life of Deborah Sampson. Write a diary entry that tells what you think might have happened to her after her secret was revealed.

## REVIEWING VOCABULARY

Match each word on the left with the correct definition on the right.

1. orderly
2. commission
3. mutiny
4. skirmish
5. hoard
6. curtly
7. torment

a. rebellion against military superiors
b. abruptly
c. a document that approves a soldier's military appointment
d. assistant to a military officer
e. great pain or anguish
f. brief fight
g. secret supply

## THINKING CRITICALLY

1. What clues does the author give you to the narrator's real identity? Look through the story to find them.
2. The narrator's decision to join the army was very risky. Had the secret been discovered, she might have been court-martialed or even executed. Why do you think Deborah Sampson took such a risk? Use details from the story to support your view.
3. Have you ever thought of warfare as "romantic"? What did you learn about war from this story?
4. How did reading this story give you a deeper understanding of the sacrifices people make for personal freedom? for their country's freedom? Explain.